The Great Tribulation

Who Shall Be Able to Stand?

Pastor Christine Peebles
Victory Temple Ministry of Reconciliation

For the great day of his wrath is come; and who shall be able to stand?
—*Revelation 6:17*

ISBN 979-8-89243-763-9 (paperback)
ISBN 979-8-89243-764-6 (digital)

Copyright © 2024 by Pastor Christine Peebles

All rights reserved. No part of this publication may be reproduced, distributed, or transmitted in any form or by any means, including photocopying, recording, or other electronic or mechanical methods without the prior written permission of the publisher. For permission requests, solicit the publisher via the address below.

Christian Faith Publishing
832 Park Avenue
Meadville, PA 16335
www.christianfaithpublishing.com

Printed in the United States of America

For then shall be great tribulation such as was not since the beginning of the world to this time, no, nor ever shall be.

—Matthew 24:21

Contents

Introduction..vii
Chapter 1: Being Patient in Tribulations 1
Chapter 2: Only the Strong Shall Survive......................18
Chapter 3: Chosen Vessels for the Great Tribulations 38
Chapter 4: The Costly Anointing 62
Chapter 5: The Great Tribulation 79
Chapter 6: Who Shall Be Able to Stand?....................101

Introduction

Talking about the great tribulation, it is not just an ordinary tribulation; Jesus describes it as being the great tribulation. We are going to have to really be in Jesus, filled and baptized with the Holy Ghost and with fire to be able to stand and endure. The Father, the Son, and the Holy Ghost—the three is one. We are living in this world, and we are going to have tribulations, and the only way that we can and will have peace is to be in Jesus and Jesus in us. The Bible said in John 16:33: "These things I have spoken unto you, that in me you might have peace. In the world you shall have tribulation; but be of a good cheer; I have overcome the world."

The Holy Ghost is a promise from our Father unto us that comes from the Lord Jesus Christ. We have got to be in a place of waiting for him. He told his disciples what to do and how to do, and today, he is telling us the same thing. The Bible said, "And, behold, I send the promise of my Father upon you: but tarry ye in the city of Jerusalem, until ye be endued with power from on high" (Luke 24:49).

John was on the isle that is called Patmos for the word of God and the testimony of Jesus Christ. John saw and wrote in a book the great tribulations that is to come. The Bible said,

> And the heaven departed as a scroll when it is rolled together; and every mountain and island were moved out of their places. And the kings of the earth, and the great men, and the rich men, and the chief captains, and the mighty men, and every bond man, and every free man, they hid

themselves in the dens and in the rocks of the mountains. And said unto the mountains and rocks, fall on us, and hide us from the face of him that sits on the throne, and from the wrath of the Lamb. For the great day of his wrath is come; and who shall be able to stand? (Revelation 6:14–17)

Chapter 1

Being Patient in Tribulations

We will never be able to have patience in tribulation except that we know what tribulation is. The Word of God will teach us how to deal with it or them. Tribulation is anguish, which is severe mental or physical pain or suffering. Anguish also is extreme pain, distress, or anxiety. Some of the things that comes with anguish are grief, heartaches, heartbreaks, misery, sorrows, sufferings, and torment. Along with tribulations also comes intense oppressions, persecutions, and great sufferings. The tribulations are going to be what is going to make God's people to be righteous again or to be restored unto God.

James tells us about the trying of our faith, and that we are to let patience have her perfect works in us. The Bible said, "My brethren, count it all joy when you fall into divers of temptations. Knowing this, that the trying of your faith worketh patience. But let patience have her perfect work, that ye maybe perfect and entire, wanting nothing" (James 1:2–4). We cannot have patience without having some tribulations; Paul tells us to glory in our tribulations. The Bible said, "And not only so, but we glory in tribulations also: knowing that tribulations worketh patience. And patience experience, and experience hope. And hope makes not ashamed; because the love of God is shed abroad in our hearts by the Holy Ghost which is given unto us" (Romans 5:3–5).

If we are making preparation to enter in the kingdom of God, then we must prepare ourselves to go through much tribulations.

PASTOR CHRISTINE PEEBLES

What is going to cause the tribulations to come forth is when we are believers, and the signs follow the believers. The Bible said in Mark 16:15–18,

> And he said unto them, go ye into the world, and preach the gospel to every creature. He that believeth and is baptized shall be saved; but he that believeth not shall be damned. And these signs shall follow them that believe; in my name shall they cast out devils; they shall speak with knew tongues. They shall take up serpents; and they shall drink any deadly thing, and it shall not hurt them; they shall lay hands on the sick, and they shall recover.

The word of God made mention of laying hands on the sick, and they shall be healed; well, apostle Paul did not lay hands, but he preached the word of faith that caused a lame man to walk. He suffered persecutions, he had tribulations, but he said that if we enter the kingdom of God, there was going to be through much tribulation. The Bible said,

> They were aware of it, and fled into Lystra, and Derbe, cities of Lycaonia, and unto the region that lieth round about. And they preached the gospel. And there sat a certain man at Lystra, impotent in his feet, being a cripple from his mother's womb, who never had walked. The same heard Paul speak: who steadfastly beholding him, and perceiving that he had faith to be healed. Said with a loud voice, stand upright on thy feet. And he leaped and walked. And there came thither certain Jews from Antioch and Iconium, who persuaded the people and having stoned Paul, drew him out of the city, supposing he had been dead. Howbeit, as the disciples

THE GREAT TRIBULATION

stood round about him, he rosed up, and come into the city: and the next day he departed with Barnabas to Derbe. And when they had preached the gospel to that city, and had taught many, they returned to Lystra, and to Iconium, and Antioch. Conforming the souls of the disciples, that we must through much tribulation enter the kingdom of God. (Acts 14:6–10, 19–22)

"Having patience, you must trust the Lord with all your heart."

To have patience, you cannot trust the Lord partially, nor can you use your natural mind for thinking. There has got to be a complete or total trust in the Lord, and the mind has got to be spiritual. Solomon said in Proverbs 3:5–6: "Trust in the Lord with all thine heart; and lean not unto thine own understanding." In all thy ways acknowledge him, and he shall direct thy paths. Paul said in Romans 12:1–2,

> I BESEECH you therefore, brethren, by the mercies of God, that ye present your bodies a living sacrifice, holy, acceptable unto God, which is your reasonable service. And be not conformed to this world; but be ye transformed by the renewing of your mind, that ye may prove what is that good, and acceptable, and perfect will of God.

When we present our bodies unto God, he purges and perfects the heart, and he transforms the mind and the thoughts. When we become crucified with Christ, he lives in us and through us. Paul said in Galatians 2:20: "I am crucified with Christ; nevertheless, I live; not I, but Christ lives in me: and the life which I now live in the flesh, I live by the faith of the Son of God, who loved me, and gave himself for me."

Job was not crucified with Christ because Christ had not come down out of heaven and entered a fleshly body to be crucified, but

Job knew that the redeemer was going to come upon the land and would come into the world. Job knew that God his Father, and his Son Jesus, were one in the Holy Spirit. Job said, "For I know that my redeemer lives, and that he shall stand for me in the latter day upon the earth. And though after my skin worms destroy this body, yet in my flesh shall I see God. Whom I shall see for myself, and mine eyes shall behold, and not another; though my reins be consumed within me" (Job 19:25–27). Job knew that his earthly body was going to be destroyed and that he would have a heavenly body. Paul said in 2 Corinthians 5:1–2: "For we know that if our earthly house of this tabernacle, were dissolved, we have a building of God, a house not made with hands, eternal in the heavens. For in this we groan earnestly desiring to be clothed upon with our house which is from heaven." Job had already done what Paul said in Romans 12:1–2.

Job had given his whole body, soul, and mind unto God; he knew that everything was going to be done away with except his soul. Job knew that it was going to be with him even as it was with David when he said, "As for me, I will behold thy face in righteousness: I shall be satisfied, when I awake with thy likeness" (Psalms 17:15). Well, David was talking about his awakening after death. Job knew that he was going to die one day. He knew that his tribulations were appointed by God, and the greatest thing that he had known was that a change was going to come, so Job asked a question, then he made a statement. The Bible said, "If a man die, shall he live again? All the days of my appointed time, will I wait until my change come" (Job 14:14). Job lived the life to be like God because he knew that one day, he was going to see God, and the way that he would recognize him would be because he would be just like him. The Bible said, "Beloved, now are we the sons of God, and it doth not yet appear what we shall be: but we know that when he shall appear, we shall be like him; for we shall see him as he is" (1 John 3:2).

"Job had patience in the midst of his tribulations."

Satan, the devil is the one that causes the tribulations to come, but when you love God with all your heart, and with all your mind, and with all your strength, which is the first commandment according to Mark 12:30, the devil cannot do nothing until he gets the per-

THE GREAT TRIBULATION

mission from God. God had an encounter with Satan as to where he was coming from; when he answered God, he gave Satan permission to attack Job. The Bible said,

> There was a day when the sons of God came to present themselves before the Lord, and Satan came also among them. And the Lord said unto Satan. Whence cometh thy? Then Satan answered the Lord and said, from going to and fro in the earth, and from walking up and down in it. And the Lord said unto Satan, Hast thou considered my servant Job, that there is none like him in the earth, a perfect and upright man, one that fears God, and escheweth evil. (Job 1:6–8)

Revelation 12:10 said, "For the accuser of our brethren is cast down, which accused them before our God, day, and night." So Satan was standing before God ready to accuse Job. The Bible went on to say,

> Then Satan answered the Lord, and said, Doth Job fear God for nought? Hast not thou made a hedge about him, and about his house, and about all that he hath on every side? Thou hast blessed the works of his hands, and his substance is increase in the land. But, put forth thine hand now, and touch all that he hath, and he will curse thee to thy face. (Job 1:9–11)

After that, God gave Satan permission and power to touch all that Job had, but he was not allowed to touch Job. The Bible went on to say, "And the Lord said unto Satan, Behold, all that he hath is in thy power; only upon himself put not forth thine hand." So Satan went forth from the presence of the Lord.

"Job have patience in tribulation."

The Bible went on to say,

> And there was a day when his sons and his daughters were eating and drinking wine in their eldest brother's house. And there came a messenger unto Job and said, The oxen were plowing, and the asses feeding beside them. And the Sabeans fell upon them, and took them away; yea, they have slain the servants with the edge of the sword; and I only have escaped alone to tell thee. While he was yet speaking, there came also another and said, The fire of God is fallen from heaven, and hath burned up the sheep, and the servants, and have consumed them; and I only am escaped alone to tell thee. While he was yet speaking, there came also another, and said, The Chaldeans made out three bands, and fell upon the camels, and have carried them away, yea, and have slain the servants with the edge of the sword; and I only am escaped alone to tell thee. While he was yet speaking, there came also another and said, Thy sons and thy daughters were eating drinking wine in their eldest brother's house. And behold, there came a great wind from the wilderness, and smote the four corners of the house, and it fell upon the house, and it fell upon the young men, and they are dead; and I only am escaped alone to tell thee. (Job 1:13–19)

Job did not fulfill the accusations of Satan, but he worshipped and blessed God. He had patience in tribulations. The Bible went on to say,

> Then Job arose, and he rent his mantle, and shaved his head, and fell upon the ground, and worshipped. And said, Naked came I out of my moth-

THE GREAT TRIBULATION

> er's womb, and naked shall I return thither: the
> Lord gave, and the Lord hath taken away; blessed
> be the name of the Lord. In all this Job sinned not,
> nor charged God foolishly. (Job 1:6–22)

Whenever we come and present ourselves before God, we better know and believe that the devil is going to be right there. The Bible tells us that the devil comes with tricks, and it tells us what to do to stand against the tricks. It is written in Ephesians 6:11–12: "Put on the whole armor of God, that ye may be able to stand against the wiles (tricks) of the devil." It is wisdom, knowledge, and understanding to know exactly what we are fighting against. The Bible went on to say, "For we wrestle not against flesh and blood, but against principalities, against powers, against the rulers of the darkness of this world, against spiritual wickedness in high places." Our warfares and our battles are not with the flesh, but we are fighting against spiritual wickedness in high places, places of principalities where darkness is ruling. We need to know the weapons of our warfare to be able to pull down the strongholds. Paul said in 2 Corinthians 10:4–5, "For the weapons of our warfare are not carnal, but mighty through God to the pulling down of strong holds. Casting down imaginations, and every high thing that exalts itself against the knowledge of God, and bringing into captivity every thought to the obedience of Christ."

"Satan comes back with more tricks for Job."

Satan has sacks filled with tricks, and he never stops pulling them out of the sack. Satan comes after what he thinks is our weakness. If he thought that Jesus had a weakness, what do you think that he is thinking about you and me? Satan knows what we are doing for God and what causes weakness in our flesh; he knows that he cannot satisfy the spiritual, and he does not want to. He is after the flesh. The weakness of Jesus's flesh was hunger, and Satan knew it—that is when his attacks began. The Bible said,

> And Jesus being full of the Holy Ghost
> returned from Jordan, and was led by the spirit
> into the wilderness. Being forty days tempted of

the devil, and in those days, he did eat nothing: and when they were ended, he afterward hungered. And the devil said unto him, If thou be the Son of God, command this stone that it be made bread. The weapon of our warfare is the word of God, and that was Jesus' weapon upon Satan.

The Bible went on to say,

> And Jesus answered him saying, It is written, That man shall not live by bread alone, but by every word of God. And the devil taking him up into a high mountain, showed him all the kingdoms of the world in a moment of time (it does not take the devil long to do what he got to do). And the devil said unto him, All this power will I give thee, and the glory of them: for that is delivered unto me; and to whomsoever I will give it. If thou therefore wilt worship me, all shall be thine. And Jesus answered and said unto him, Get thee behind me Satan; for it is written, Thou shalt worship the Lord thy God, and him only shalt thy serve. And he brought him to Jerusalem and set him on a pinnacle of the temple, and said unto him, If thou be the Son of God, cast thyself down from hence. For it is written, 'He shall give his angels charged over thee, to keep thee. And in their hands, they shall bear thee up, lest at any time thou dash thy foot against a stone. And Jesus answering said unto him, it is said, Thou shalt not tempt the Lord thy God. And when the devil had ended all the temptations, he departed from him for a season. (Luke 4:1–13)

Satan came back to Job with more and knew tricks. The Bible said that he departed from Jesus for a season, meaning that he left,

THE GREAT TRIBULATION

but most definitely he would be back. After his tricks failed with Job, he departed for a season, then he returned. The Bible said,

> Again, there was a day when the sons of God came to present themselves before the Lord, and Satan came also among them to present himself before the Lord. (Whenever we pray, Satan is there). And the Lord said unto Satan, From whence cometh thou? And Satan answered the Lord and said, From going to and fro in the earth and from walking up and down in it. The Lord said unto Satan, Hast thou considered my servant Job, that there is none like him in the earth, a perfect and upright man, one that fears God, and escheweth evil? And still he holds fast his integrity, although thou moved me against him, to destroy him without cause. And Satan answered the Lord and said, Skin for skin, yea, all that a man hath will he give for his life. But put forth thine hand now, and touch his bone and his flesh, and he will curse thee to thy face. And the Lord said unto Satan, Behold, he is in thine hand; but save his life. So went forth Satan from the presence of the Lord, and smote Job with sore boils from the sole of his foot unto his crown. Sometimes love ones and family will leave or forsake us, but Jesus said in Hebrews 13:5: I will never leave thee, nor will I forsake thee. Job's wife was ready to forsake him. She rather to see him dead than see him being patient in tribulation.

The Bible went on to say,

> And he took him a potsherd to scrape himself withal: and he sat down among the ashes. Then said his wife unto him, Dost thy still retain

thine integrity? Curse God and die. Job knew that he had to have patience in the midst of his tribulations, so, he told his wife: But he said unto her, Thou speaks as one of the foolish women speaks. What? Shall we see good at the hand of God, and shall we not receive evil? In all this did not Job sin with his lips. (Job 2:1–10)

Job could have patience in tribulations because he already knew what life held for him: a whole lot of troubles, or a life filled with troubles. He said in Job 14:1: Man that is born of a woman is of a few days, and full of trouble. Life is going to be filled with troubles, but when we are in God, and God is in us, he is going to order our steps, and if we fall, he is going to pick us up and not forsake us. The Bible said, "The steps of a good man is ordered by the Lord: and he delights in his way. Though he fall, he shall not be utterly cast down; for the Lord upholds him with his hand. I have been young, and now am old; yet have I not seen the righteous forsaken nor his seed begging bread" (Psalms 37:23–25). David knew that whatever God had spoken, it was sealed and settled in heaven, so he said in Psalms 119:89: "Forever, O Lord, thy word is settled in heaven." David knew that he needed a light upon the path that he was taking, so he said in Psalms 119:105: "Thy word is a lamp unto my feet, and a light unto my path." David knew that the word of God was established in heaven, and the word was a lamp unto his feet and a light unto his path, so he asked the Lord in Psalms 119:133: "Order my steps in thy word: and let not any iniquity have dominion over me." Before David had said unto God and asked of God, he knew that he could not have sin working in his life, and that only the word of God could deliver him out of sin, so he said in Psalms 119:11: "Thy word have I hid in mine heart, that I might not sin against thee."

Job's steps were ordered by the Lord, and he knew that whatever he had to go through was going to be appointed by God and not Satan. He knew that patience was going to bring on some tribulations, and in tribulations, he could not do anything but wait on the Lord to move in his stead; so he said in Job 14:14:

THE GREAT TRIBULATION

> If a man die, shall he live again? All the days of my appointed time will I wait until my change come. Thou shalt call, and I will answer thee: thou wilt have a desire to the work of thine hands. For now, thou number my steps: dost thy not watch over my sin? My transgression is sealed up in a bag, and thy sews up my iniquity.

Job knew that he had to wait upon the Lord, and no matter what type valley he was in, or how tall the mountains were, and the crooked and rough places were, he knew that God would fix it, for

> Every valley shall be exalted, and every mountain and hill shall be made low: and the crooked shall be made straight, and the rough places plain. But they that wait upon the Lord shall renew their strength; they shall mount up with wings as eagles: they shall run and not be weary; they shall walk, and not faint. (Isaiah 40:4 and 31)

Job did not want the mountains and hills and the valleys and the rough and the crooked places to cause him to be weary in his running nor cause him to faint in his walk with God. Job gave the more honest heed to what Paul had said in Galatians 6:9: "And let us not be weary in well doing: for in due season, we shall reap if we faint not." Job did not faint, he had patience in tribulations.

"Job's patience in tribulation caused his captivity to turn."

Job's focus was not on the things that was happening unto him and around him. He done as it was written in Colossians 3:2: "Set your affections on those things above, not on things on the earth." Job was seeking after the things that comes from above; that is what he was after the most. He knew what the trying of his faith was going to turn into, so Job went on to say unto God, "But he knows the way that I take: when he hath tried me, I shall come forth as gold."

Job's three friends were grieved over his conditions or his having patience in tribulations, so they went to try to help him to bear his griefs, which was to no avail because they were not in a rightful place with God.

Those three men did as the church folk are doing today: They flowed with the show. The Bible said,

> Now when Job three friends heard of all this evil that was come upon him, they came everyone from his place: Eliphaz the Temanite, and Bildad the Shunite, and Zophar the Naamathite: for they all had made an appointment together to come to mourn with him and to comfort him. And when they lifted their eyes afar off, and knew him not, they lift their voices, and wept; and they rent everyone his mantle, and sprinkled dust upon their heads toward heaven. So, they sat down with him upon the ground seven days and seven nights and none spoke a word unto him; for they saw that his grief was very heavy. (Job 2:11–13)

Job's three friends might have mourned and wept with him, but God did not hear their prayers because they had not spoken of the things that were right like Job had. Job, in the time of his tribulations, had to pray for them. The Bible said,

> And it was so that after the Lord had spoken those words unto Job, the Lord said to Eliphaz the Temanite, My wrath is kindled against thee, and thy two friends; for ye have not spoken of me the things that is right as my servant Job hath. Therefore, take unto you now seven bullocks and seven rams, and go to my servant Job, and offer up for yourselves a burnt offering; and my servant Job shall pray for you: for him shall I accept: lest I

THE GREAT TRIBULATION

deal with you after your folly, in that ye have not spoken of me the things which is right, like my servant Job. So Eliphaz the Temanite, and Bildad the Shuhite, and Zophar the Naamathite went and did according as the Lord commanded them; the Lord also accepted Job. (Job 42:7–9)

When we wait patiently in the times of tribulations, pay day is going to come, especially when we know that we are children of God. Our sufferings are not worthy to be compared with what God is going to do. Apostle Paul said in Romans 8:16–18,

> The Spirit itself bears witness with our spirit that we are the children of God. Then if children, then heirs; heirs of God, and joint hairs with Christ; if so be that we suffer with him, that we may be also glorified with together. For I reckon that the suffering of this present time is not worth to be compared with the glory which shall be revealed in us.

"Job received double for his troubles."

Now, Paul said that we cannot compare our sufferings with the glory of God; it is not possible. Most definitely, Job's sufferings could not be compared with God's glory. Job received double for his troubles. The Bible said,

> And the Lord turned the captivity of Job when he prayed for his friends: also, the Lord gave Job twice as much as he had before. Then came there unto him all his brethren, and all his sisters, and all they that had been of his acquaintance before, and did eat with him in his house, and the bemoaned him, and comforted him over all the evil that the Lord had brought upon him: every man also gave him a piece of money, and

everyone an earring of gold. So, the Lord blessed the latter end of Job more than his beginning: for he had fourteen thousand sheep, and six thousand camels, and a thousand yoke of oxen, and a thousand she asses. He had also seven sons and three daughters. And he called the name of the first, Jemima; and the name of the second, Kezia; and the name of the third, Karen-happuch. And in all the land were no women found so fair as the daughters of Job; and their father gave them inheritance among their brethren. After this lived Job a hundred and forty years, and saw his sons, and his son's sons, even four generations. So, Job died, being old and full of days. (Job 42:10–17)

"Having patience in tribulation is to be in Christ Jesus."

When Jesus is in us and we are in him, we are going to have patience in tribulation because Jesus is our beginning, and he is our ending; he is the author and the finisher of our faith. To run and to stay in the race, we have got to do it with patience. The Bible said,

WHEREFORE SEEING we also are compassed about with so great a cloud of witnesses, let us lay aside every weight, and the sin which doth so easily beset us, and let us run with patience the race that is set before us. Looking unto Jesus the author and the finisher of our faith; who for the joy that was set before him endured the cross, despising the shame, and is set down at the right hand of the throne of God. For consider him that endured (had patience) such contradiction of sinners against himself, lest ye be wearied and faint in your minds. Ye have not yet resisted unto blood striving against sin. And ye have forgotten the exhortation which speaks unto you as unto children, my son, despise not the chastening of

THE GREAT TRIBULATION

the Lord, nor faint when thou art rebuked of
him. For whom the Lord loveth he chastens and
scourges every son who he receives. If you endure
chastening, God deals with you as with sons; for
what son is he whom the father chastens not?
But if ye be without chastisement, whereof all
are partakers, then are ye bastards and not sons.
Further-more we have had fathers of our flesh
which corrected us, and we gave them reference:
shall we not much rather be in subjection to the
Father of spirits and live? For they verily for a few
days chastened us after their own pleasure; but he
for our profit, that we might be partakers of his
holiness. (Hebrews 12:1–10)

As Jesus Christ had patience in tribulation, enduring and suffering in his flesh, he commands that his people do likewise. The Bible said, "FORASMUCH THEN as Christ hath suffered for us in the flesh, arm yourselves likewise with the same mind: for he that hath suffered in the flesh hath ceased from sin; that he no longer should live the rest of his time in the flesh to the lusts of men, but to the will of God" (1 Peter 4:1–2).

Jesus having patience in tribulations, his sufferings were for the sins of the people, not only for the just, but it was for the unjust as well. Jesus had not come into the world to suffer for God's people when the Bible said,

And God saw that the wickedness of man
was great in the earth, and that every imagination
of the thoughts of his heart was only evil continually. And it repented the Lord that he had made
man on the earth, and it grieved him at his heart.
And the Lord said, I will destroy man whom I
have created from the face of the earth; both man
and beast and the creeping thing, and the fowls

of the air; for it repented me that I have made them. (Genesis 6:5–7)

God destroyed the first world for the exception of eight people—Noah, his wife, his three sons and his three daughters-in-law, and two of every living creature and animals, male and female. As the world repopulated, and sin waxed worse, the conclusion was drawn that animal's blood could not take away sins. God saw a need for the world to have a savior. God sent his Son Jesus down from heaven to get into a fleshly body, to suffer and to have patience in tribulation. This is what Jesus said,

For it is not possible that the blood of bulls and of goats should take away sins. Wherefore when he cometh into the world, he saith sacrifice and offering thou would not, but a body has thou prepared me. In burnt offerings and sacrifices for sin thou hast had no pleasure. Then said I, Lo, I come in the volume of the book, it is written of me, to do thy will O God. Above when he said, Sacrifice and offering and burnt offerings and offerings for sin, thou would not, neither have pleasure therein; which are offered by the law. Then said he, Lo, I come to do thy will, O God. He taketh away the first that he may establish the second. By the which will we are sanctified through the offering of the body of Jesus Christ once for all. And every priest standing daily ministering and offering oftentimes the same sacrifices, which can never take away sins. But this man, after he had offered one sacrifice for sins forever, sat down on the right hand of God. From henceforth expecting till his enemies be made his footstool. For by one offering he hath perfected for ever them that are sanctified. Whereof the Holy Ghost also is a witness to us; for after that

THE GREAT TRIBULATION

> he had said before. This is the covenant that I will make with them after those days, saith the Lord, I will put my laws into their hearts, and in their minds will I write them. And their sins and iniquities will I remember no more. Now, where remission of these is, there is no more offering for sin. (Hebrews 10:4–18)

As it has been said, Jesus had patience in tribulations, he suffered long, having no respect of persons; he suffered afflictions for the whole world. He did not forget about those people of the first world who had died and went to hell before he came on the scene. After his sufferings and endurance, and his death, and they buried him in a grave. They had watchmen at his grave because they had heard him say that he was going to rise again in three days, and they thought that his disciples would come and steal his body. Little did they know that while they were guarding his grave, Jesus was not in it, but he had gone down into hell to preach to the spirits, the souls that were in hell. The Bible said,

> For it is better if the will of God be so, that ye suffer for well doing, than for evil doing. For Christ also hath once suffered for sins, the just for the unjust, that he might bring us to God, being put to death in the flesh, but quickened by the Spirit. By which also he went and preached unto the spirits in prison. Which sometime were disobedient, when once the long suffering of God waited in the days of Noah, while the ark was a-preparing, wherein few, that is, eight souls were saved by water. (1 Peter 3:17–20)

"Being patient in tribulation is going to come forth by Jesus Christ living on the inside of us, which is the baptism of the Holy Ghost with fire" (Matthew 3:11).

Chapter 2

Only the Strong Shall Survive

When John was on the isle that is called Patmos to get the word of God and the testimony of Jesus Christ that God told John in Revelation 1:11: "I am Alpha and Omega, the first and the last; and what thou see, write in a book, and send it to the seven churches which are in Asia." Jesus the Lion out of the Tribe of Judah, the Root of David, opened the book and began to lose the seven seals, which is the seven wraths and judgments of God. John asked a question in Revelation 6:17: "For the great day of his wrath is come; and who shall be able to stand? Only the strong shall survive."

Talking about only the strong surviving, God is not talking about nor is he requiring our physical strength; he is talking about a spiritual strength and to be strong in him. With a physical strength and some equipment, we can remove natural mountains. The mountains that are in our lives, they are spiritual, and only faith in God can remove them. Jesus's disciples had an encounter with a man and his son who had a spiritual mountain, and they did not have what it took to remove that mountain, and they wondered why they could not remove the mountain, but Jesus opened their understanding and gave them the knowledge that they needed. The Bible said,

> And when they were come to the multitude, there came to him a certain man kneeling down to him and saying, Lord, have mercy on my son:

THE GREAT TRIBULATION

for he is a lunatic, and vexed: for often he falls into the fire, and often into the water. And I brought him to thy disciples, and they could not cure him. Then Jesus answered and said, O faithless and perverse generation, how long shall I be with you? How long shall I suffer you? Bring him thither to me. And Jesus rebuked the devil; and he departed out of him: and the child was cured that very hour. Then came the disciples to Jesus apart, and said, Why could not we cast him out? And Jesus said unto them, Because of your unbelief: for verily I say unto you, if you have faith as a grain of mustard seed, ye shall say unto this mountain, Remove hence to yonder place, and it shall remove, and nothing shall be impossible unto you. Howbeit, this kind goes out by prayer and fasting only.

(Prayer and fasting are where our spiritual strength comes from.) (Matthew 17:14–21)

Apostle Paul was talking to the saints that were at Ephesus, letting them know that they had been chosen to be blessed with spiritual blessings in heavenly places. The Bible said,

PAUL AN apostle of Jesus Christ by the will of God, to the saints which are at Ephesus, and to the faithful in Christ Jesus. Grace be unto you, and peace from God our Father, and from the Lord Jesus Christ. Bless be the God and Father of our Lord Jesus Christ, who hath blessed us with spiritual blessings in heavenly places in Christ. According as he has chosen us in him before the foundation of the world that we should be holy and without blame before him in love. Having predestinated us unto the adaption of children by Jesus Christ to himself according to the good pleasure of his will. To the praise of the glory of his grace, wherein he hath made us accepted in the beloved. In whom we have redemption through his blood, the forgiveness of sins, according to the riches of his grace. (Ephesians 1:1–7)

Paul could see where the church had gone to sleep (spiritually) and was drunken in the days that were evil, so he said unto the saints,

Wherefore he saith, Awake thou that sleeps, and arise from the dead, and Christ shall give you the light. See then that you walk circumspectly, not as fools, but as wise. Redeeming the time, because the days are evil. Wherefore be ye not unwise, but understanding what the will of the Lord is. And be not drunk with wine, wherein is excess; but be filled with the Spirit. (Ephesians 5:14–18)

Only the strong shall survive. After apostle Paul talked to the saints who were at Ephesus, or before he concluded, he made them to know that they had to be strong in the Lord, and that was going to be the only way that they would be able to survive. In his conclusion, he used the word *finally*. The Bible said, "Finally, my brethren, be strong in the Lord, and in the power of his might." Since Paul has told us to be strong in the Lord, he does not leave us hanging, he tells us what we got to do to be strong, and to stand against the tricks of the devil. The Bible said,

Put on the whole armor of God, that ye may be able to stand against the wiles (tricks) of the devil. You will never be able to overcome or be strong except you know what you are fighting or wrestling against. Sometimes we think that it is that man, that woman, that boy, or that girl; no, it is not them, we are in a spiritual warfare.

THE GREAT TRIBULATION

The Bible went on to say,

> For we wrestle not against flesh and blood, but against principalities, against powers, against the rulers of the darkness of this world, against spiritual wickedness in high places. This is an evil day that we are living in, and God want us to be strong, and do all we can to stand.

The Bible went on to say,

> Stand therefore having your loins girt about with truth, and having on the breastplate of righteousness. And your feet shod with the preparation of the gospel of peace. Above all, taking the shield of faith, wherewith ye shall be able to quench all the fiery darts of the wicked. And take the helmet of salvation, and the sword of the spirit, which is the word of God. Not any of the armors of God are going to work in us or through us without prayers and supplications.

The Bible went on to say, "Praying always with prayer and supplication in the Spirit, and watching there unto with all perseverance and supplication for saints" (Ephesians 6:10–18).

Now that we know that we have got to put on the whole armor of God to be strong and to stand against the tricks of the devil. We need to know how and what we are going to fight with. In a spiritual warfare, we cannot be carnal; carnality will destroy or kill us. The carnal mind, which is the fleshly mind, hates God; and if we hate God, then he cannot fight for us. Bottom line, his spirit does not live in us, and if his spirit does not live in us, then we cannot be strong in him. If we are not strong in the Lord, we are going to die a spiritual death. God talked to Adam in the Garden of Eden about death. Adam did not know that God was talking about a spiritual death. There are two deaths, natural and spiritual. A natural death separates the soul from the body. A spiritual death separates the soul from God. The Bible said in Genesis 15–17:

> And the Lord God took the man, and put him into the garden of Eden to dress it and to keep it. And the Lord commanded the man saying, of every tree of the garden thou mayest freely eat: but of the tree of the knowledge of good and evil, thou shalt not eat of it: for in the day that thou eat thereof thou shalt surely die.

Nakedness represents death. When the devil deceived Adam and Eve to eat of the tree of the knowledge of good and evil, that is when they discovered that they were naked, which was a spiritual death. The Bible said,

> And when the woman saw that the tree was good for food and that it was pleasant to the eyes, a tree to make one wise, she took of the tree thereof, and did eat, and gave also to her husband with her: and he did eat. And the eyes of them both were opened, and they knew that they were naked; and they sewed fig leaves together, and made themselves aprons. Nakedness or spiritual death will make you run from God. God is above, and he looks down and he sees and knows it all.

The Bible went on to say,

> And they heard the voice of the Lord walking in the garden in the cool of the day; and Adam and his wife hid themselves from the presence of the Lord amongst the trees of the garden. And the Lord God called unto Adam, and said unto him, Where art thou? And he said I heard

THE GREAT TRIBULATION

thy voice in the garden, and I was afraid because I was naked; and I hid myself. Again, God is above, and he looks down and sees and he knows it all.

The Bible went on to say,

> And he said, Who told thee that thou was naked? Have thou eaten of the tree, whereof I command thee that thou shouldest not eat? Adam blaming someone else for his downfall or his disobedience unto God, that spirit is still roaming around in the world and upon the land today.

The Bible went on to say, "And the man said, The woman who thou gave to be with me, she gave me of the tree, and I did eat. And the Lord God said unto the woman, What is this that thou hast done? And the woman said that the serpent beguiled me, and I did eat" (Genesis 3:6–13).

Adam caused sin and death to come upon us all. It is said in Romans 5:12: "Wherefore, as by one man sin entered the world, and death by sin; and so, death passed upon all men, for that all have sinned."

Even as Adam died a spiritual death, we were all born spiritually dead. That is why Jesus told Nicodemus that he must be born again. Jesus also put a distinct between the flesh and the spirit. The Bible said,

> THERE WAS a man of the Pharisees, named Nicodemus, a ruler of the Jews. The same came to Jesus by night, and said unto to him, Rabbi, we know that thou art a teacher come from God: for no man can do these miracles that thou do except God be with him. Jesus answered and said unto him, Verily, verily, I say unto thee, Except a man be born again, he cannot see the kingdom of God. Nicodemus saith unto him, How can a man

> be born when he is old? Can he enter the second time into his mother's womb, and be born? Jesus answered, verily, verily, I say unto thee, Except a man be born of the water and of the Spirit, he cannot enter into the kingdom of God. That which is born of the flesh is flesh; that which is born of the Spirit is Spirit. Marvel not that I said unto thee, Ye must be born again. (John 3:1–7)

When a man is born again, he obtains a spiritual mind, and a spiritual mind gives him life, and a carnal mind gives him death. A spiritual mind comes from Christ Jesus, and of course, the fleshly mind is the mind that we were born with, which condemns us. Paul said in Romans 8:15, "There is therefore now no condemnation to them which are in Christ Jesus, who walk not after the flesh, but after the Spirit. For the law of the Spirit of life in Christ Jesus hath made me free from the law of sin and death." Paul lets us know that if we are after the flesh, we will do the things that are fleshly, and if we are after the Spirit, we will do the things that are spiritual, and the things that are spiritual is what will or shall please God. The Bible went on to say,

> For they that are after the flesh do mind the things of the flesh; but they that are after the Spirit, the things of the Spirit. For to be carnally minded is death; but to be spiritually minded is life and peace. Because the carnal mind is enmity against God: for it is not subject to the law of God, neither indeed can be. So, they that are in the flesh cannot please God.

Now we know to be strong in the Lord; we have got to fight. The outward man wars and fight against the inward man. The outward man is the flesh, and the inward man is Jesus Christ, the Spirit of God living in our souls, which is a forever and an ongoing battle,

THE GREAT TRIBULATION

but the victor and the overcomer is he who lives on the inside of us. It is written in 1 John 4:4–6:

> Ye are of God little children, and have overcome them, because greater is he that is in you, than he that is in the world. They are of the world: therefore, speak they of the world, and the world heareth them. We are of God: he that knows God heareth us; he that is not of God hears not us. Hereby know We the spirit of truth, and the spirit of error.

"Strength is the weapon to pull down strongholds."

We are in a spiritual warfare, and even as Paul said, we are not wrestling against flesh and blood, but we are wrestling against principalities. Principalities are the authorities of the rulers and governments, which we the Christians are subject to or do abide by their rules. It is said in Titus 3:1: "PUT THEM in mind to be subject to principalities and powers to obey magistrates, to be ready to every good work."

It is ordained by God that our souls be subject unto the higher powers, but also, we have got to render unto all, that which is due to them, that we will owe no man nothing but to love them. The Bible said in Romans 13:1–8:

> LET EVERY soul be subject unto the higher powers. For there is no power but of God: the power that be are ordained of God. Whosoever therefore resists the power, resists the ordinance of God: and they that resist shall receive to themselves damnation. For the rulers are not a terror to good works, but to the evil. Wilt thou then not be afraid of the power? Do that which is good and thou shalt have praise of the same. For he is the minister of God for good. But if thou do that which is evil, be afraid; for he bears not the

sword in vain; for he is the minister of God, a revenger to execute wrath upon him that doth evil. Wherefore ye must needs to be subject, not only for wrath, but also for conscience sake. For this cause pay ye tribute also: for they are God's ministers, attending continually upon this very thing. Render therefore all their dues: custom to whom custom: fear to whom fear: honor to whom honor. Owe no man anything but to love one another; for he that loves another hath fulfilled the law.

God wants us to obey them that have rule over us because they are the ones that watches over our souls. The Bible said, "Obey them that have the rule over you, and submit yourselves: for they watch for your souls, as they that must give account, that they must do it with joy, and not with grief: for that is unprofitable for you" (Hebrews 13:17).

The Lord wants the church to know about the principalities and the powers in heavenly places that was from the beginning. The Bible said,

Unto me who am lest than the least of all saints, is this grace given, that I should preach among the Gentiles the unsearchable riches of Christ. And to make all men see what is the fellowship of the mystery, which from the beginning of the world hath been hid in God, who created all things by Jesus Christ. To the intent that now unto the principalities and powers in heavenly places might be known by the church the manifold wisdom of God. (Ephesians 3:8–10)

Jesus, the Holy Ghost, is our comforter and our keeper. We overcome all things by and with his precious blood. We know that God created the heavens and the earth, and he created the principal-

THE GREAT TRIBULATION

ities. He is the head of the church—not only of the church but of all things as well. The Bible said,

> For by him were all things created, that are in heaven, and that are in earth, visible, and invisible, whether they be thrones or dominions, or principalities, or powers, all things were created by him and for him. And he is before all things, and by him all things consist. And he is the head of the body, the church who is the beginning, the first born from the dead; that in all things he might have the preeminence. (Colossians 1:16–18)

Jesus forgives us for our sins by blotting out the handwriting that was against us and nailing them to the cross and causing us to triumph over them. The Bible said,

> In whom also ye are circumcised with the circumcision made without hands, in putting of the body of the sins of the flesh by the circumcision of Christ. Buried with him in baptism, wherein also ye are risen with him through the faith of the operation of God, who hath raised him from the dead. And you, being dead in your sins and in the uncircumcision of your flesh, hath he quickened together with him, having forgiven you all trespasses. Blotting out the handwriting of ordinances that was against us, and took it out of the way, nailing it to his cross. And having spoiled principalities and powers, he made a show of them in it. (Colossians 2:11–15)

God wanted us to know and believe that Jesus Christ is above all principalities in this world and in the world to come. The Bible said,

> That the God of our Lord Jesus Christ, the Father of glory, may give unto you the spirit of

wisdom and revelation in the knowledge of him. The eyes of your understanding be enlightened; that ye may know what is the hope of his calling, and what the riches of the glory of his inheritance in the saints. And what is the exceeding greatness of his power to us-ward who believe, according to the working of his mighty power. Which he wrought in Christ, when he raised him from the dead, and set him at his own right hand in heavenly places. For above all principalities, and power, and might, and dominion, and every name that is named, not only in this world, but also in that which is to come. And put all things under his feet, and gave him to be the head over all things to the church. Which is the body, the fulness of him that fills all in all. (Ephesians 1:17–23)

With the powers and the principalities, we are accounted as sheep for the slaughter. We are killed all day long, but we are more than conquerors, and none of these things shall separate us from the love of God. The Bible said,

Who shall separate us from the love of Christ? Shall tribulation, or distress, or persecution, or famine, or nakedness, or peril, or sword? As it is written, For thy sake, we are killed all the day long: we are accounted as sheep for the slaughter. Nay, in all these things we are more than conquerors through him that loved us. For I am persuaded, that neither death, nor life, nor angels, nor principalities, nor powers, nor things present, nor things to come, nor height, nor depth, nor any other creature, shall be able to separate us from the love of God, which is in Christ Jesus our Lord. (Romans 8:35–39)

THE GREAT TRIBULATION

Yes, we are in the flesh, and we are walking in the flesh, but as Paul said in Ephesians 6:12, we wrestle not against flesh and blood. We are in a spiritual warfare, and we cannot fight with a carnal weapon. A carnal weapon cannot pull down strongholds. Strongholds such as thoughts and imaginations cannot be touched physically because they are spirits. Therefore, a spiritual warfare cannot be fought with a carnal weapon; the weapons of our warfare are going to be spiritual. The Bible said,

> For though we walk in the flesh, we do not war after the flesh. (For the weapons of our warfare are not carnal, but mighty through God to the pulling down of strongholds.). Casting down imaginations, and every high thing that exalts itself against the knowledge of God, and bringing into captivity every thought to the obedience of Christ. (2 Corinthians 10:3–5)

"The weapon of our warfare is the word of God."

The word of God has been here ever since the beginning of the world. God did not come down from heaven and made things into exitance; God did it with the speaking of his word. The Bible said, "In the beginning was the word, and the word was with God, and the word was God. The same was in the beginning with God. All things were made by him; and without him was not anything made that was made (John 1:1–3).

Everything that has been done, everything that is being done, and everything that shall be done are by the word of God. Nothing can be done in this world without the word of God. There is nothing that can move as fast as the word of God; there is nothing as powerful as the word of God. There is nothing that is as sharp as the word of God; there is nothing that can discern the thoughts and the intents of the heart but the word of God. The Bible said, "The word of God is quick, and powerful, and sharper than any two-edge sword, piercing even to the dividing asunder of soul and spirit, and of the joints and marrow, and is a discerner of the thoughts and intents of the heart" (Hebrews 4:12). When John was on the isle called Patmos to get the word of God and the testimony of Jesus Christ, he saw where the word of God went out of Jesus's mouth a sharp two-edged sword. The Bible said, "And he had in his right hand seven stars; and out of his mouth went a sharp two-edged sword; and his countenance was as the sun shineth in his strength" (Revelation 1:16).

God, his word, and the Holy Ghost bear record in heaven. The Bible said, "For there are three that bear record in heaven, the Father, the Word, and the Holy Ghost: and these three are one" (1 John 5:7). Jesus is the word of God. The Bible said, "And he was clothed with a vesture dipped in blood: and his name is called the word of God" (Revelation 19:13).

Apostle Paul made mention of pulling down strongholds and imaginations that exalt themselves against the knowledge of God. This is a spiritual warfare that is going to take the word of God to pull down those strongholds. We do not have to go to heaven to get the word of God; in fact, we are going to need the word of God to get to heaven. We will not have to try to go down into the deep, nor try raising Christ from the dead again. Where does the word of God ought to be? In our mouths and in our hearts. David said in Psalms 119:11, "Thy word have I hid in mine heart, that I might not sin against thee." Apostle Paul told us in the word of God what we do not have to do, and where the word of God is. The Bible said,

> But the righteousness which is of faith speaks on this wise, Say not in thine heart, Who shall ascend into heaven? That is to bring Christ down from above. Or who shall descend into the deep? That is to bring Christ again from the dead. But what saith it? The word is nigh thee, even in thy mouth, and in thy heart: that is, the word of faith, which we preach. That if thou shalt confess with thy mouth the Lord Jesus, and shalt believe in thine heart that God hath raised him from the dead, thou shalt be saved. For with the heart man believes unto righteousness; and

THE GREAT TRIBULATION

with the mouth confession is made unto salvation. (Romans 10:6–10)

"The word is given unto the strong to root out, pull down, and to destroy."

The Lord talked to Jeremiah when he was only a child, letting him know the works that he had ordained that he do. God knows all about us, and he knew about us before we were born. God knows the strength that we have and that we do not even know about and the things that we do have the ability to do and not to do. Therefore, he gives according to our abilities. The Bible said in Matthew 25:15, "And unto one he gave five talents, to another two, and to another one; to every man according to his several abilities; and straight took his journey."

When Jeremiah was a child, God put his word in his mouth, and he told him what to do with the word. He told him to root up, to pull down, and to destroy. The prophets of today are rooting up, pulling down, and destroying. After God told Jeremiah to do all those things, it was not in his plan for him to leave everything desolate. He told Jeremiah to build and to plant. The Bible said,

Before I formed thee in the belly, I knew thee; and before thou came forth out of the womb, I sanctified thee and I ordained the to be a prophet unto the nations. Then said I, Ah Lord God! Behold, I cannot speak: for I am a child. But the Lord said unto me, Say not I am a child: for thou shalt go to all that I shall send thee, and whatsoever I command thee thou shalt speak. Be not afraid of their faces: for I am with thee to deliver thee saith the Lord. Then the Lord put forth his hand, and touched my mouth. And the Lord said unto me, Behold, I have put my words in thy mouth. See I have this day set thee over the nations and over the kingdoms, to root out and

to pull down, and to destroy, and to throw down,
to build and to plant. (Jeremiah 1:4–10)

Jeremiah was one of God's major prophets. He had to stand in the gap for the children of Israel. God showed Jeremiah the falling away of Israel. And how they were doing their own thing or, more so, establishing their own righteousness. Paul talked about what Israel had done in Romans 10:1–3:

> BRETHREN MY heart desire and prayer, to God for Israel is that they might be saved. For I bear them record that they have a zeal of God, but not according to knowledge. For they being ignorant of God's righteousness, and going about to establish their own righteousness, have not submitted themselves unto the righteousness of God. Our righteousness was spoken of in Isaiah 64:6: But we are all as an unclean thing, and all our righteousness are as filthy rags; and we do fade as a leaf: and our iniquities like the wind, have taken us away.

Israel was God's bride, but the bride had left him, and he wanted her to return unto him, so he said in Jeremiah 3:14–15: "Turn O backsliding children, saith the Lord; for I am married unto you; and I will take you one of a city, and two of a family, and will bring you to Zion. And I will give you pastors according to mine heart, which will feed you with knowledge and understanding."

"God shows and tells Jeremiah that Israel has to be made over again."

Now, God tells Jeremiah where to go to hear his words and how he would make Israel over again. Only the strong shall survive. The Bible said,

> THE WORD which came to Jeremiah from the Lord, saying, Arise, and go down to the pot-

THE GREAT TRIBULATION

ter's house, and there I will cause thee to hear my words. Then I went down to the potter's house, and behold, he wrought a work on wheels. And the vessel that he had made of clay was marred in the hand of the potter: so, he made it again, another vessel, as seemed good to the potter to make it. Then the word of the Lord came unto me saying, O house of Israel, cannot I do with you as the potter, saith the Lord. Behold, as the clay is in the potter's hand, so are ye in my hand, O house of Israel.

Now, God is about do through Jeremiah what was spoken if in Jeremiah chapter 1. The Bible went on to say,

In what instant shall I speak concerning a nation, and concerning a kingdom, to pluck up, and to pull down, and to destroy. If that nation against whom I have pronounced, turn from their evil, I will repent of the evil that I thought to do unto them. And at what instant I shall speak concerning a nation, and concerning a kingdom, to build and to plant it. (Jeremiah 18:1–10)

"The word of God was the weapon of Jeremiah's warfare."

When you have the word of God inside you, the word of God is going to be the weapon of your warfare. Your enemies are going to perform weapons against you, but their weapons cannot defeat God's word that is on the inside of you. We have got to do as David said in Psalms 119:11: "Thy word have I hid in mine heart, that I might not sin against thee." When you choose to speak and obey the word of God, the devil desires to destroy you and get rid of you forever; he wants to kill you, but at the same time, Jesus comes to give us life. The Bible said, "The thief comes not, but for to kill and to steal, and to destroy: I am come that they might have life, and that they may have it more abundantly. The devil comes to kill, to steal, and to destroy, but whatever weapon he uses, it is not going to work." It is said in Isaiah 54:17, "No weapon that is formed against thee shall prosper; and every tongue that shall rise against thee in the judgment thou shalt condemn. This is the heritage of the servants of the Lord, and their righteousness is of me saith the Lord."

Immediately after God has spoken a word unto you, and you walk in obedience thereto, the devil is coming to try to kill and destroy you, but when the word of God is hidden in our heart, it is not going to happen. God told Jeremiah to go and speak to the men of Judah and the inhabitants of Jerusalem to turn from their wicked ways. The Bible said,

> Now therefore go to speak to the men of Judah, and to the inhabitants of Jerusalem, saying, Thus saith the Lord; Behold, I frame evil against you, and devise a device against you: return ye now everyone from his evil way; and make your ways and your doings good. And they said, there is no hope: but we will walk after our devices, and we will everyone do the imaginations of his evil heart. Therefore, thus saith the Lord; Ask ye now among the heathens, who hath heard such things; the virgin of Israel hath done a very horrible thing. Will a man leave the snow of Lebanon, which comes from the rock of the field? Or shall the cold flowing waters that comes from another place be forsaken? Because my people have forgotten me, they have burned incense to vanity, and they have caused them to stumble in their ways from the ancient paths, to walk in paths, in a way not cast up. To make their land desolate, and a perpetual hissing; everyone that passes thereby shall be astonished, and wag his head. I will scatter them as with an east wind before the enemy; I will show them the back, and not the face, in the day of their calamity. The people did

THE GREAT TRIBULATION

not want to hear the words of the Lord, so, they wanted to shut Jeremiah's mouth, and not hear what God had to say.

The Bible went on to say,

> Then said they, Come, and let us devise devices against Jeremiah; for the law shall not perish from the priest, nor counsel the wise, nor the word from the prophet. Come, and let us smite him with the tongue, and let us not give heed to any of his words. Jeremiah questioned God about being recompensed evil for the good that he had done.

The Bible went on to say, "Shall evil be recompensed for good? For they have dug a pit for my soul. Remember that I stood before thee to speak good for them, and to turn away the wrath from them" (Jeremiah 18:11–20).

Jeremiah felt as if he had been made a mockery, so he told God, "I am just not going to speak in your name anymore." He tried that, but it did not work because the word of God was burning in his heart. The Bible said,

> O Lord, thou hast deceived me, and I was deceived; thou art stronger than I, and hast prevailed: I am in derision daily, everyone mocks me. For since I spoke, cried out, I cried violence and spoil; because the word of the Lord was made a reproach unto me, and a derision daily. When the word of God began to burn in Jeremiah's heart, he knew then that only the strong shall survive. His enemies were prepared to take their revenge on him, but he knew that the Lord was with him, and that his enemies would not prevail.

The Bible went on to say,

> Then said I, I will not make mention of him, nor speak any more in his name. but his word was in mine heart as a burning fire shut up in my bones, and I was weary with forbearing, and I could not stay. For I heard the defaming of many, fear on every side. Report said they, and we will report it. All my familiars watched for my halting, saying, Peradventure he will be enticed, and we shall prevail against him, and we shall take our revenge on him. But the Lord is with me as a mighty terrible one: therefore, my persecutors shall stumble, and they shall not prevail: they shall be greatly ashamed; for they shall not prosper: their everlasting confusion shall never be forgotten. But, O Lord of hosts, that tries the righteous, and sees the reins and the heart, let me see thy vengeance on them: for unto thee I have opened my cause. Sing unto the Lord, praise ye the Lord: for he hath delivered the soul of the poor from the hand of evildoers. (Jeremiah 20:7–13)

"Strength comes from the word of God."

The word and God are the same as God and Jesus; therefore, the words *God* and *Jesus* cannot be separated. The Bible said in John 1:1: "IN THE beginning was the word, and the word was with God, and the word was God." Jesus is the Holy Ghost who comes to live in our souls. He is the one who said in Revelation 3:20: "Behold, I stand at the door and knock: if any man shall hear my voice, and open the door, I will come in to him, and will sup with him, and he with me." He also said in 1 John 5:7: "For there are three that bear record in heaven, the Father, the Word, and the Holy Ghost: and those three are one."

THE GREAT TRIBULATION

The word of the Lord is where our strength is going to come from. Solomon said in Proverbs 18:10: "The name of the Lord is a strong tower: the righteous runs into it, and is safe."

"Only the strong shall survive."

Chapter 3

Chosen Vessels for the Great Tribulations

For the great tribulation, God will not choose just anybody. God cannot use people that are in love with the world because if they are in love with the world, then they do not love God. God is seeking for a people who is strong in the knowledge of his word and who loves him and not the world. The Bible said,

> I write unto you fathers, because ye have known him that is from the beginning, I write unto you young men, because ye have overcome the wicked one. I write unto you little children, because ye have known the Father. I have written unto you fathers, because ye have known him that was from the beginning; I have written unto you young men because ye are strong, and the word of God abides in you, and ye have overcome the wicked one. Love not the world, neither the things that are in the world. If any man loves the world, the love of the Father is not in him. For all that is in the world, the lust of the flesh, and the lust of the eyes, and the pride of life, is not of the Father, but of the world. And

THE GREAT TRIBULATION

the world passes away, and the lust thereof; but he that doeth the will of God abides forever. (1 John 2:13–17)

It is not the outward man nor the flesh that God want us to present unto him. Paul said that there is nothing good in our flesh, and with the flesh evil is always present, and there is a continual warfare in our members waring against the laws of our minds, to captivate the sin in our members. The Bible said,

For I know that in me, (that is, in my flesh), dwelleth no good thing: for the will is present with me; but how to perform that which is good I find not. For the good I would do I do not: but the evil which I would not, that I do. Now if I do that I would not, it is no more I that do it, but sin that dwelleth in me. I find then a law, that when I would do good, evil is present with me. For I delight in the law of God after the inward man. But I see another law in my members, warring against the law of my mind, and bringing me into captivity of the law of sin which is in my members. O wretched man that I am! Who shall deliver me from the body of this death? I thank God through Jesus Christ our Lord. So then with the mind, I, myself serve the law of God; but with the flesh, the law of sin. (Romans 7:18–25)

Everything that God does, he does it on the inside of us; even his light will shine on the inside of us. He put his treasures on the inside of his vessels. The Bible said,

For God who commend the light to shine out of darkness, hath shinned in our hearts, to give the light of the knowledge of the glory of God in the face of Jesus Christ. But we have this treasure in earthen vessels, that the excellency of the power may be in God, and not of us. We are troubled on every side, yet not distressed; we are perplexed, but not in despair. Persecuted, but not forsaken, cast down but not destroyed. Always bearing about in the body the dying of the Lord Jesus, that the life also of Jesus might be made manifest in our body. For we which live are always delivered unto death for Jesus' sake that the life also of Jesus might be made manifest in our mortal flesh. So, then death worketh in us, but life in you. We having the same spirit of faith, according as it is written, I believed, and therefore have I spoken. Knowing that he which raised up the Lord Jesus shall raise us up also by Jesus, and shall present us with you. For all things are for your sakes, that the abundant grace, might through the thanksgiving of many redound to the glory of God. For which cause, we faint not; but though our outward man perishes, yet the inward man is renewed is renewed day by day. For our light affliction, which is for but a moment, worketh for us a far more exceeding and eternal weight of glory. While we look not at the things which are seen, but at the things that are not seen; for the things which are seen are temporal; but the things which are not seen are eternal. (2 Corinthians 4:6–18)

The chosen vessels that God shall have and use in the great tribulations are going to present their whole body, mind, and soul unto God. No vessel is going to think of himself more highly than what he ought. The Bible said in Ephesians 4:16, "From whom the whole body fitly joined together and compacted by that which every joint supplies, according to the effectual working in the measure of every part maketh increase of the body unto the edifying of itself in love."

THE GREAT TRIBULATION

The vessels are going to know that the body has many members; the gifts are different, but all shall operate by faith. The Bible said,

> I BESEECH you therefore, brethren, by the mercies of God, that ye present your bodies a living sacrifice, holy acceptable unto God, which is your reasonable service. And be not conformed to this world: but be ye transformed by the renewing of your mind, that ye may prove what is that good, and acceptable and perfect will of God. For I say, through the grace given unto me, to every man that is among you, not to think of himself more highly than he ought to think; but to think soberly, according to how God hath dwelt to every man the measure of faith. For as we have many members in one body, and all members have not the same office. So, we being many, are one body in Christ, and everyone members one of another. Having the gifts differing according to the grace that is given to us, whether prophecy, let us prophesy according to the proportion of faith. Or ministry, let us wait on our ministry; or he that teaches, on teaching. Or he that exalts, on exaltation: he that giveth let him do it with simplicity; him that rules with diligence; he that shows mercy, with cheerfulness. Let love be without dissimulation. Abhor (hate) that which is evil; cleave to that which is good. Be kindly affectionate one to another with brotherly love; in honor preferring one another. (Romans 12:1–10)

"The vessels that does not obey God, he will remove them."

If you do not obey God, he can or will quickly remove you. He said I will let the stones take your place. It is written in Matthew 19:40: "And he answered and said unto them, I tell you that, if they should hold their peace, the stones would immediately cry out."

PASTOR CHRISTINE PEEBLES

Sometimes, when people are in certain places or positions, they have the tendency to thank that they cannot be replaced. In the Bible, there was a king whose name was Ahasuerus; he had a beautiful queen whose name was Vashti. She thought that her being in the king's palace, and the king looked on her as being a beautiful lady who could do as she pleased. The is the same thing that happens unto a lot of God's people. God began to raise them up and use them, then they began to think that they do not have to obey God, nor his word, nor them he made to be ruler over them. God spoke about his chosen vessels in 1 Peter 2:9–10:

> But ye are a chosen generation, a royal priesthood, and a holy nation, a peculiar people: that he should show forth the praises of him who hath called you out of darkness into his marvelous light. Which in time pass was not a people, but now are the people of God: which had not obtained mercy, but now have obtained mercy.

Queen Vashti just knew that she had it made, and that she was not replaceable. As people now refuse to do what God asks them to do, she refused to do what King Ahasuerus told her to do. The Bible said,

> On the seventh day, when the heart of the king was merry with wine, he commanded Mehaman, Biztha, Harbona, Bigtha, and Abagtha, Zethar, and Curcas, the seven chamberlains that served in the presence of Ahasuerus the king. To bring Vashti the queen before the king with crown royal, to show the people and the princes her beauty, for she was fair to look on. But the queen Vashti refused to come at the king's commandment by his chamberlains; therefore, was the king very wroth, and his anger burned in him.

THE GREAT TRIBULATION

Vashti had the type of spirit that would cause her to fall or even be destroyed. She was sitting and walking in a high position. She had a haughty spirit and a spirit of pride. Solomon spoke about a haughty spirit and a spirit of pride and how it is better to be humble. The Bible said, "Pride goes before destruction, and a haughty spirit before a fall. Better it is to be of a humble spirit with the lowly, than to divide the spoil with the proud" (Proverbs 16:18–19). The greatest wraths and judgments can come upon us when we begin to do things that God hates. To be exalted in pride is one of the seven things that God hates. The Bible said, "These six things doth God hate: yea, seven are an abomination unto him. A proud look, a lying tongue, and hands that shed innocent blood. A heart that devises wicked imaginations, feet that be swift in running to mischief. A false witness that speaks lies, and sews discord among brethren" (Proverbs 6:16–19).

Vashi the queen possessed pride and a haughty spirit, which did not affect her alone but the king, the princes, their wives, and the other women as well. The princes knew that something had to be done about Vashti's actions and her disobedience. The Bible went on to say,

> Then the king said to the wise men, which knew the times, (for so was the king's manner toward all knew law and judgment.) And the next unto him was Carshena, Shethar, Admatha, Tarshish, Meres, Marsena, and Memucan, the seven princes of Media, which saw the king's face, and which sat the first in the kingdom. What shall we do unto the queen Vashti according to law, because she hath not performed the commandment of the king Ahasuerus by the chamberlains? And Memucan answered before the king and the princes, Vashti the queen hath not done wrong to the king only, but also to all the princes, and to all the people that are in all the provinces of the king Ahasuerus. For this deed of the queen shall come abroad unto all women, so

that they shall despise their husband in their eyes, when it shall be reported, The king Ahasuerus, commanded Vashti the queen to be brought in before him, but she came not. Likewise, shall the ladies of Persia and Media say this day unto the king's princes, which have heard of the deed of the queen. Thus shall there arise to much contempt and wrath. If it please the king, let there go a royal commandment from him, and let it be written among the laws of the Persians and the Medes, that it be not altered. That Vashti come, no more before the king Ahasuerus; and let the king give her royal estate to another that is better than she. And when the king's decree that he shall make shall be published through out all his empire, (for it is great) all the wives shall give to their husbands, honor, both to great and small. And the saying pleased the king and the princes, and the king did according to the word of Memucan. For he sent letters into all the king's provinces, into every province according to the writing thereof, and to every people and their language, that every man should bear rule in his own house, and that it should be published according to the language of every people. (Esther 1:10–22)

"The beautiful lady was replaced by another beautiful lady."

When we think that we have it all together and our ways does not please God, quickly, he can remove us and replace us with someone else who can get the job done and please God. The Bible said in Esther 2:4: "And the let the maiden which pleases the king be queen instead of Vashti. And the thing pleases the king, and he did so." The Bible said,

THE GREAT TRIBULATION

Now in Shushan the palace there was a certain Jew, whose name was Mordecai, the son of Jair, the son of Shimei, the son of Kish, a Benjamite. Who had been carried away from Jerusalem with the captivity which had been carried away with Jeconiah, king of Judah, whom Nebuchadnezzar the king of Babylon had carried away. And he brought up Hadassah that is Esther, his uncle's daughter: for she had neither father nor mother, and the maid was fair and beautiful; whom Mordecai, when her father and mother were dead, took for his own daughter. So it came to pass, when the king's commandment and his decree was heard, and when many maidens were gathered, unto Shushan the palace, to the custody of Hegai, keeper of the women. And the maiden pleased him and she obtained kindness of him; and he speedily gave her the things for her purification, with such things as belonged to her, and seven maidens, which were meet to be given her out of the king's house: and he preferred her and her maids unto the best place of the house of the women. Esther had not shown her people nor her kindred: for Mordecai had charged her that she should not show it. And Mordecai walked every day before the court of the women's house, to know how Esther did, and what should become of her. Now, when every maid's term was come to go in to king Ahasuerus, after that she had been twelve months, according to the manner of the women, (for so were the days of their purification accomplished, to wit, six months with oil of myrrh, and six months sweet odors, and with other things for the purifying of the women.) Then thus came every maiden unto the king; whatsoever she desired was given her to go with her out of the house of the women unto the king's house. In the evening she went, and on the morrow she returned into the second house of the women, to the custody of Shaashgaz, the king's chamberlain, which kept the concubines: she came in unto the king no more, except the king delighted in her, and that she was called by name. Now when the term of Esther, the daughter of Abihail the uncle of Mordecai, who had taken her for his daughter, was come to go in unto the king, she required nothing but what Hegai the king's chamberlain, the keeper of the women, appointed. And Esther obtained favor in the sight of all them that looked upon her. So, Esther was taken unto king Ahasuerus into his house royal in the tenth month, which is the month Tebeth, in the seventh year of his reign. And the king loved Esther above all the women, and she obtained grace and favor in his sight more than all the virgins; so that he set the royal crown upon her head, and made her queen instead of Vashti. (Esther 2:4–17)

"Mordecai, a chosen vessel to stand in the gap for the Jews in a time of great tribulation."

King Ahasuerus had a prince who became angry with Mordecai, and knowing that he was a Jew, he wanted to destroy him and all the Jews. In the king's palace, that prince was above all the king's princes. The Bible said in Esther 3:1: "AFTER THESE things did king Ahasuerus promote Haman the son of Hammedatha the Agagite, and advanced him, and set his seat above all the princes that were with him."

Being the people of God, we do not need to rejoice when the devil attacks another saint; he is out to kill and destroy us all. Haman found out that Mordecai was a Jew. He did not want to destroy him only; he wanted to destroy all the Jews. The Bible said,

THE GREAT TRIBULATION

Now it came to pass, when they spoke daily unto him, and he hearkened not unto them, that they told Haman, to see whether Mordecai's matters would stand: for he had told them that he was a Jew. And when Haman saw that Mordecai bowed not, nor did him reverence, then was Haman full of wrath. And he thought scorn to lay hands on Mordecai alone; for they had shown him the people of Mordecai: wherefore Haman sought to destroy all the Jews that were throughout the whole kingdom of Ahasuerus, even the people of Mordecai. In the first month, that is the month of Nisan, in the twelfth year of king Ahasuerus, they cast Pur, that is, the lot, before Haman from day to day, and from month to month, to the twelfth month, that is, the month Adar. And Haman said unto king Ahasuerus, there is a certain people scattered abroad and dispersed among the people in all the provinces of thy kingdom; and their laws are diverse from all people; neither keep they the king's laws: therefore, it is not for the king's profit to suffer them. If it please the king, let it be written that they be destroyed: and I will pay ten thousand talents of silver to the hands of those that have the charge of the business, to bring it into the king's treasuries. And the king took his ring from his hand, and gave it unto Haman, the son of Hammedatha the Agagite, the Jews' enemy. And the king said unto Haman, The silver is given to thee, the people also, to do to them as it seems good to thee. Then, were the king's scribes called on the thirteenth day of the first month, and there was written according to all that Haman had commanded unto the king's lieutenants, and to the governors that were over every province, and to the rulers of every people of every province according to the writing thereof, and to every people after their language; in the name of king Ahasuerus was it written, and sealed with the king's ring. And the letters were sent by posts into all the king's provinces, to destroy, to kill, and to cause to perish, all Jews, both young and old, little children and women, in one day, even upon the thirteenth day of the twelfth month, which is the month Adar, and to take the spoil of them for a prey. The copy of the writing for a commandment to be given to every province was published unto all people, that they should be ready against that day. The posts went out, being hastened by the king's commandment, and the decree was given in Shushan the palace. And the king and Haman sat down to drink; but the city Shushan was perplexed. (Esther 3:4–15)

"Mordecai stood in the gap for the people of God."

Chosen vessels listen to and for the voice of the Lord, and when they hear his voice, they will yield thereto. Prayer is our main source, but some things are not going to happen nor will the yoke be destroyed without some fasting. Jesus told his disciples in Matthew 17:21: "Howbeit this kind goes not out but by prayer and fasting." Fasting and praying is what will bring forth the anointing to take away the burden and destroy the yoke. It is written in Isaiah 10:27: "And it shall come to pass in that day, that his burden shall be taken away from off thy shoulder, and his yoke from off thy neck, and the yoke shall be destroyed because of the anointing."

Mordecai did what he knew would reach and touch God. He was not trying to reach God just for himself only but also for all the Jews. The Bible said,

When Mordecai perceived all that was done, Mordecai rent his clothes, and put on sack-

THE GREAT TRIBULATION

cloth with ashes, and went out into the midst of the city, and cried with a loud and bitter cry. And came even before the king's gate: for none might enter in the king's gate clothed with sackcloth. And in every province, whithersoever the king's commandment and his decree came, there was great mourning among the Jews, and fasting and weeping, and wailing; and many lay in sackcloth and ashes. Esther was in a royal place and palace, and she did not understand that Mordecai was standing in the gap for her and all the Jews that were about to be destroyed.

The Bible went on to say,

So, Esther's maids and her chamberlains came and told her. Then was the queen exceedingly grieved, and she sent raiment to clothed Mordecai, and to take away his sackcloth from him: but he received it not. Then called Esther for Hatach, one of the king's chamberlains, whom he had appointed to attend upon her, and gave him a commandment to Mordecai, to know what it was, and why it was. So Hatach went forth to Mordecai unto the street of the city, which was before the king's gate. And Mordecai told him of all that had happened unto him, and of the sum of the money that Haman had promised to pay to the king's treasuries for the Jews, to destroy them. Also, he gave him the copy of the writing of the decree that was given at Shushan to destroy them, to show it unto Esther, and to declare it unto her, and to charge her that she should go in unto the king to make supplication unto him for her people. And Hatach came and told Esther the words of Mordecai. Esther did not realize the seriousness of the matter, and that all the Jews, including herself, was about to be destroyed. She looked at her position in the king's palace, and not the fact thar she would lose the position and her life; therefore, she went on to give Mordecai commands.

The Bible went on to say,

> And Esther spoke unto Hatach, and gave him commandment unto Mordecai. And the king's servants, and the people of the king's province, do know, that whosoever, whether man or woman, shall come unto the king into the inner court, who is not called, there is one law of his to put him to death, except such to whom the king shall hold out the golden scepter, that he may live: but I have not been called to come in unto the king these thirty days. And they told to Mordecai Esther's words. God does not choose vessels according to how they look, walk, nor talk. God choose vessels and put them in places that he can be used for deliverance for his people. In the temple or palace, there is always light. God put Esther in the temple to be that light.

The Bible went on to say,

> Then Mordecai commanded to answer Esther, Think not with thyself that thou shalt escape in the king's house, more than all the Jews. For if thou altogether hold thy peace at this time, then shall their enlargement and deliverance arise to the Jews from another place; but thou and thy father's house shall be destroyed: and who knows

THE GREAT TRIBULATION

whether thou art come to the kingdom for such a time as this?

"Esther hearkens to the voice of God through Mordecai."

Mordecai was able to reach Esther when he reminded her that she was a Jew, and that she would not be exempted from being destroyed. She knew that she could be put to death if she went before the king, and she was not called. So she called for three days and nights of fasting with all the Jews that were at Shushan. Solomon said in Ecclesiastes 8:4: "Where the word of a king is, there is power: and who may say unto him, what doeth thou?"

Well, Esther said, "I will go unto the king, and if I perish, I perish." The Bible went on to say,

> Then Esther bade them return Mordecai this answer. Go gather all the Jews that are present in Shushan, and fast ye for me, and neither eat nor drink three days, night or day: I also and my maidens will fast likewise; and so, will I go in unto the king, which is not according to the law: and if I perish, I perish. So, Mordecai went his way, and did according to all that Esther had commanded him. (Esther 4:4–17)

After Esther, Mordecai, and the people had fasted three days and three nights, she put on her royal apparel; and she went to see the king. Haman went to his wife Zeresh and all his friends. Haman's wife told his friends that they would make gallows, then they would go to see the king about hanging Mordecai. The Bible said,

> Now it came to pass on the third day, that Esther put on her royal apparel, and stood in the inner court of the king's house, over against the king's house: and the king sat upon his royal throne in the royal house, over the gate of the house. And it was so, when the king saw Esther

PASTOR CHRISTINE PEEBLES

the queen standing in the court, that she obtained favor in his sight: and the king held out to Esther the golden scepter that was in his hand. So, Esther drew near, and touched the top of the scepter. Then said the king unto her, What wilt thou, queen Esther? And what is thou request? It shall be even given thee to the half of the kingdom. And Esther answered, if it seems good unto the king, let the king and Haman come this day unto the banquet that I have prepared for him. Then the king said, Cause Haman to make haste, that he may do as Esther hath said. So, the king and Haman came to the banquet that Esther had prepared. And the king said unto Esther at the banquet of wine, What is thy petition? And it shall be granted thee: and what is thy request? Even to the half of the kingdom it shall be performed. Then answered Esther, and said, My petition and my request is: If I have found favor in the sight of the king, and if it please the king, to grant my petition, and perform my request, let the king and Haman come to the banquet that I shall prepare for them, and I will do tomorrow as the king hath said. Then went Haman forth that day joyful and with a glad heart: but when Haman saw Mordecai in the king's gate, that he stood not up, nor moved for him, he was full of indignation against Mordecai. Nevertheless, Haman refrained himself: and when he came home, he sent and called for his friends, and Zeresh his wife. And Haman told them of the glory of his riches, and the multitude of his children, and all the things wherein the king had promoted him, and how he had advanced him above the princes and servants of the king. Haman said moreover, Yea, Esther the queen did let no man come in

THE GREAT TRIBULATION

> with the king unto the banquet that she had pre-
> pared but myself: and tomorrow am I invited
> unto her also with the king. Yet all this avails me
> nothing, so long as I see Mordecai the Jew sitting
> at the king's gate. Then said Zeresh his wife and
> all his friends unto him, Let a gallows be made of
> fifty cubits high, and tomorrow speak thou unto
> the king that Mordecai may be hanged thereon;
> then go therein merrily with the king unto the
> banquet. And the thing pleased Haman, and he
> cause the gallows to be made. (Esther 5:1–14)

"The chosen vessels for the great tribulation, shall stand, and the wicked shall be destroyed."

The chosen vessels for the great tribulations are going to stand, and they are going to have peace in the times of the tribulations. They will be even as Paul said in Philippians 4:6–7: "Be careful for nothing; but in everything by prayer and supplication and with thanksgiving, let your request be made known unto God. And the peace of God, which passes all understanding, shall keep your hearts and minds through Christ Jesus."

I heard some words in a song that said, "If you dig one ditch, you better dig two because the next one just might be for you." My saying is, if you dig on ditch, you want need to dig two because the first one is going to be for you. That is the way it was when Haman had gallows built to hang Mordecai; he was hanged with the same gallows. The Bible said,

> So, THE king and Haman came to the ban-
> quet with Esther the queen. And the king said
> again unto Esther on the second day of the ban-
> quet of wine, What is thy petition, queen Esther?
> And what shall be granted thee: and what is thy
> request? And it shall be performed, even to the
> half of the kingdom. Then Esther the queen
> answered and said, If I have found favor in thy

PASTOR CHRISTINE PEEBLES

sight, O king, and if it please the king, let my life be given me at my petition, and my people at my request. For we are sold, I and my people, to be destroyed, to be slain, and to perish. But if we had been sold for bondmen and bondwomen, I had held my tongue, although the enemy could not countervail the king's damage. Then the king Ahasuerus answered and said unto Esther the queen, Who is he, and where is he, that durst presume in his heart to do so? And Esther said The adversary and enemy is this wicked Haman. Then Haman was afraid before the king and the queen. And the king arising from the banquet of wine in his wrath went into the palace garden: and Haman stood up to make request for his life to Esther the queen; for he saw that there was evil determined against him by the king. Then the king returned out of the palace garden into the place of the banquet of wine; and Haman was fallen upon the bed whereon Esther was. Then said the king, Will he force the queen also before me in the house? As the word went out of the king's mouth, they covered Haman's face. And Harbonah, one of the chamberlains, said before the king, Behold, also, the gallows fifty cubits high, which Haman had made for Mordecai, who had spoken good for the king, stands in the house of Haman. So, they hanged Haman on the gallows that he had prepared for Mordecai. Then was the king's wrath pacified. (Esther 7:1–10)

"Saul, apostle Paul, was a chosen vessel for a time of tribulations."

I have noticed that some people who do such wicked and evil doings, those are the ones that God will choose to do might works in him. Not only that, but he chooses people who are unlearned. God cannot use people who already know everything. When a per-

THE GREAT TRIBULATION

son seems to already know everything, that is a spirit of pride. Pride sets a person up to be resisted by God. The Bible said in James 4:6: "But he giveth more grace. Wherefore he saith, God resist the proud, but he gives grace unto the humble."

God has a way to make us know how to humble ourselves. Saul was headed to a place of bringing great tribulations upon the saints of God, but Jesus had a way of stopping and humbling him. The Bible said,

> AND SAUL, yet breathing out threatening, and slaughter against the disciples of the Lord, went unto the high priest. And desired of him letters to Damacus to the synagogues, that if he found any of this way, whether they were men or women, he might bring them bound into Jerusalem. And as he journeyed, he came near Damacus: and suddenly, there shinned round and about him a light from heaven. And he fell to the earth, and heard a voice saying unto him, Saul, Saul, why persecutes thou me? And he said who art thou Lord? I am Jesus whom thou persecutes: it is hard for thee to kick against the pricks. (Acts 9:1–5)

When Jesus got Saul's attention, the first thing that he wanted to know was what Jesus wanted him to do. The Bible went on to say, "And he trembling and astonished said, what wilt thou have me to do? And the Lord said unto him, Arise, and go into the city, and it shall be told thee what thou must do. And the men which journeyed with him stood speechless, hearing a voice, but seeing no man." The Lord had to close Saul's eyes that he might lose sight of the things of this world and see the things of him. The Bible went on to say,

> And Saul arose from the earth, and when his eyes were opened, he saw no man: but they led him by the hand, and brought him into

Damascus. And he was three days without sight, and neither did eat nor drink. And there was a certain disciple at Damacus, named Ananias, and to him said the Lord in a vision, Ananias. And he said, Behold, I am here, Lord. And the Lord said unto him, Arise and go into the street which is called straight, and inquire in the house of Judas for one called Saul, of Tarsus: for, behold, he prays. And hath seen in a vision a man name Ananias coming in, and putting his hand on him, that he might receive his sight. (Acts 9:8–12)

Ananias began to talk to the Lord about the things that he had heard about Saul and what he was doing unto the saints. God forgives, and he does not see things as man sees them. We look from the outside, and God looks on the inside. The Bible said in 1 Samuel 16:7, "For the Lord sees not as man sees; for he looks on the outward appearance, but the Lord looks on the heart." The Bible went on to say, "Then Ananias answered, Lord, I have heard by many of this man, how much evil he hath done to thy saints at Jerusalem. And here he hath authority from the chief priests to bind all that call on thy name."

Thanks and glory be unto God that man cannot make choices as to whom shall be the chosen vessels of the Lord; it is the Lord that does that and him only. The Bible went on to say, "But the Lord said unto him, Go thy way; he is a chosen vessel unto me, to bear my name before the Gentiles and kings, and the children of Israel. For I will show him how great things he must suffer for my name's sake."

"Saul received his sight and the baptism of the Holy Ghost."

Once Saul received his sight and the baptism of the Holy Ghost, then he could see clearly the things of God. He was ready to preach the gospel of Jesus Christ and to fulfill the call of a chosen vessel. The Bible went on to say,

And Ananias went his way, and entered the house; and putting his hands on him said,

THE GREAT TRIBULATION

Brother Saul, the Lord, even Jesus, that appeared unto thee in the way as thou came, hath sent me, that thou mightiest receive thy sight, and be filled with the Holy Ghost. And immediately there fell from his eyes as it had been scales; and he receive sight forthwith, and arose, and was baptized. And when he had received meat, he was strengthened. Then was Saul certain days with the disciples which was at Damacus. And straightway he preached Christ in the synagogues, that he is the Son of God. But all that heard him were amazed, and said; Is not this he that destroyed them which called on this name in Jerusalem, and came hither for that intent, that he might bring them bound unto the chief priest? But Saul increased the more in strength, and confound the Jews which dwelt at Damacus, proving that this is very Christ. And after that many days were fulfilled, the Jews took counsel to kill him. Being a vessel for the great tribulation, the devil is going to be out to kill and destroy you; and that was the situation with Saul, but God had a way of escape made for him, and he is going to have a way escape made for us.

The Bible went on to say,

But their laying await was known of Saul. And they watched the gates day and night to kill him. Then the disciples took him by night, and let him down by the wall in a basket. And when Saul was come to Jerusalem, he assayed to join himself to the disciples: but they were all afraid of him, and believed not that he was a disciple. But Barnabas took him, and brought him to the apostles, and declared unto them how he had seen the Lord in the way, and that he had spoken to him, and how he had preached boldly at Damacus in the name of Jesus. And he was with them coming in and going out at Jerusalem. And he spoke boldly in the name of the Lord Jesus, and disputed against the Grecians: but they went about to slay him. Which when the brethren knew, they brought him down to Caesarea, and sent him forth to Tarsus. Then had the churches rest throughout all Judaea and Galilee, and Samaria, and were edified, and walking in the fear of the Lord, and in the comfort of the Holy Ghost, were multiplied. (Acts 9:17–31)

"A chosen vessel suffers for the namesake of Christ."

A chosen vessel will suffer for the namesake of Christ, but a way of escape shall be made. Paul said in 1 Corinthians 10:13: "There hath no temptation taken you but such as is common to man: but God is faithful, who will not suffer you to be tempted above that ye are able; but will with the temptation also make a way to escape, that ye may be able to bear it."

Paul had an encounter with a demonic spirit of divination. In Jesus's name he cast the demon out. The people of Macedonia became angry with Paul and Silas. They beat them and put them in prison; Paul and Salis sang and prayed their way out. The Bible said,

And it came to pass, as we went to prayer, a certain damsel, possessed with a spirit of divination met us, which brought her masters much gain by soothsaying. The same followed Paul and us, and cried, saying, These men are the servants of the most high God, which show unto us the way of salvation. And this did she many days: but Paul being grieved, turned, and said to the spirit, I command thee in the name of Jesus Christ to come out of her. And he came out the same hour.

THE GREAT TRIBULATION

And when her masters saw that the hope of their gains were gone, they caught Paul and Silas, and drew them into the marketplace unto the rulers. And brought them to the magistrates, saying, These men, being Jews, do exceedingly trouble our city. And teach customs, which are not lawful for us to receive, neither observe, being Romans. And the multitude rose together against them: and the magistrates rent off their clothes, and commanded to beat them. And when they had laid many stripes upon them, they cast them into prison, charging the jailer to keep them safely. Who, having received such a charge, thrust them into the inner prison, and made their feet fast in the stocks. And at midnight Paul and Silas prayed, and sang praises unto God; and the prisoners heard them. And suddenly there was a great earthquake, so that the foundations of the prison were shaken: and immediately all the doors were opened, and every one's bands were loosed. And the keeper of the prison awakening out of his sleep, and seeing the prison doors open, he drew out his sword, and would have killed himself, supposing that the prisoners had been fled. But Paul cried with a loud voice, saying, Do thyself no harm: for we are all here. Then he called for a light, and sprang it, and came trembling, and fell down before Paul and Silas. And brought them out, and said, sirs, what must I do to be saved? And they said, Believe on the Lord Jesus Christ, and thy shall be saved, and thy house. And they spoke unto him the word of the Lord, and to all that were in his house. And he took them the same hour of the night, and washed their stripes; and was baptized, he and all his, straightway. And when he had brought them into the house, he set meat before them, and rejoiced, believing in God with all his house. And when it was day, the magistrates sent the sergeants, saying, Let those men go. And the keeper of the prison told this saying to Paul, The magistrates have sent to let you go: now therefore depart, and go in peace. But Paul said unto them, They have beaten us openly uncondemn, being Romans, and have cast us into prison; and now do they thrust us out privily? Nay verily; but let them come themselves and fetch us out. And the sergeants told these words unto the magistrates; and they feared, when they heard that they were Romans. And they came and besought them, and brought them out, and desired them to depart out of the city. And they went out of the prison, and entered the house of Lydia: and when they had seen the brethren, they comforted them, and departed. (Acts 16:16–40)

For the great tribulations, the vessels that God is going to use, they will be chosen by God. As it was with apostle Paul, he was chosen by God, and he suffered many things for the namesake of Christ. Almost at the end of Paul's journey, he had this testimony: "I have fought a good fight, I have finished my course, I have kept the faith. Henceforth there is laid up for me a crown of righteousness, which the Lord, the righteous judge, shall give me at that day: and not to me only, but unto all them also that love his appearing" (2 Timothy 4:6–8).

A Chosen Vessel for the Great Tribulation

On October 8, 2023, Sunday, God made it known unto me that I am a chosen vessel for the great tribulation. I was preaching and revealing the revelations of Jesus Christ that were revealed to John when he was on the isle of Patmos. The Lord allowed the same thing to happen to me as he did Saul when he was on the road to

THE GREAT TRIBULATION

Damascus, and a light shined from heaven round and about him. I was preaching and praying for people on the church parking lot when the Lord let a light from heaven shine down on me. That light let me know that I am a chosen vessel for the great tribulation.

Chapter 4

The Costly Anointing

Talking about the costly anointing that can be compared with what Solomon said about a virtuous woman, the Bible said,

> Who can find a virtuous woman? For her price is far above rubies. The heart of her husband doth safely trust in her, so then he shall have no need of spoil. She will do him good and not evil all the days of her life. She seeks wool, and flax, and works willingly with her hands. She is like the merchant's ships: she brings her food from afar. She rise also while it is night, and gives meat to her household, and a portion to her maidens. She considers a field, and buys it: with the fruit of her hands, she plants a vineyard. She girds her loins with strength, and strengthen with her arms. She perceives that her merchandise is good: her candle goes not out by night. She lays her hands to the spindle, and her hands hold the distaff. She stretches out her hands to the poor; yea, she reaches forth her hands to the needy. She is not afraid of the snow for her household: for all her household is clothed with scarlet. She maketh herself coverings of tapestry; her clothing

THE GREAT TRIBULATION

is silk and purple. Her husband is known in the gates, when he sits among the elders of the land. She makes fine linen and sells it; and delivers girdles unto the merchants. Strength and honor are her clothing; and she shall rejoice in time to come. She opens her mouth with wisdom; and her tongue is the law of kindness. She looks well to the ways of her household, and eats not the bread of idleness. Her children arise up, and call her blessed; her husband also, and he praises her. Many daughters have done virtuously, but thou excelled them all. Favor is deceitful, and beauty is vain: but a woman that fears the Lord, she shall be praised. Give her of the fruit of her hands; and let her own works praise her in the gates. (Proverbs 31:10–31)

Jesus is the beginning and the originator of the costly anointing. There had to be the shedding of blood and death. Jesus done many mighty works when he walked upon the earth in a fleshly body, but his anointing could not come upon or within us until after his death. The Bible said,

How much more shall the blood of Christ, who through the eternal spirit offered himself without spot to God? And for this cause, he is the mediator of the New Testament, that by means of death, for the redemption of the transgressions that were under the first testament, they which are called might receive the promise of eternal inheritance. For where a testament is, there must also of necessity be the death of a testator. The testament is of force after men are dead: otherwise, it is of no strength at all while the testator lives. Whereupon neither the first testament was dedicated without blood. (Hebrews 9:14–18)

"Mary helps to prepare Jesus for his burial with a costly ointment of spikenard."

Mary was helping to prepare Jesus for his burial after death, but she did not know exactly what she was doing. Judas Iscariot came against what Mary was doing, but Jesus made him to know exactly what was going on. The Bible said,

> THEN JESUS six days before the Passover came to Bethany, where Lazarus was which had been dead, whom he raised from the dead. There they made him a supper; and Martha served: but Lazarus was one of them that sat at the table with him. Then took Mary a pound ointment of spikenard, very costly, and anointed the feet of Jesus, and wiped his feet with her hair: and the house was filled with odor of the ointment. Then said one of his disciples, Judas Iscariot, Simon's son, which should betray him. Why was not this ointment sold for three hundred pence, and given to the poor? Then he said, not that he cared for the poor: but because he was a thief, and had the bag, and bare what was put therein. Then said Jesus, Let her alone: against the day of my burying hath she kept this. For the poor always ye have with you; but me ye have not always. (John 12:1–8)

"The yoke shall be destroyed because of the anointing."

No anointing, no yoke shall be destroyed; it shall be destroyed because of the anointing. The anointing also takes away the burden off our shoulders and the yoke off our necks. It is written in Isaiah 10:27: "And it shall come to pass in that day, that his burden shall be taken away from off thy shoulder, and his yoke from off thy neck, and the yoke shall be destroyed because of the anointing." We have got to know where and whom the anointing come from. We have got to know and learn about him, the anointed one who paid the costly price. Jesus let us know in his word that no man knows him but his

THE GREAT TRIBULATION

Father, and no man knows his Father but him, and whomsoever he will reveal unto his Father. Jesus extends an invitation that we will get to know him and learn about him and that he will make our yoke easy and our burdens light. The Bible said,

> All things are delivered unto me of my Father: and no man knows the Son, but the Father, neither knows any man the Father save the Son, and he to whomsoever the Son will reveal him. Come unto me, all that labor and are heavy laden, and I will give you rest. Take my yoke upon you, and learn of me; for I am meek and lowly in heart; and ye shall find rest unto your souls. For my yoke is easy, and my burden is light. (Matthew 11:27–30)

The anointing of God is very costly; there is not enough money in the whole world to purchase the anointing. In fact, the anointing cannot be purchased with money; it is purchased with the precious blood of Christ, the Lamb of God. Peter said,

> Forasmuch as ye know that ye were not redeemed with corruptible things, as silver and gold, from your vain conversation received by tradition from your father. But with the precious blood of Christ, as of a lamb without blemish and without spot. Who verily was foreordained before the foundation of the world, but was manifest in these last times for you. Who by him do believe in God, that raised him from the dead, and gave him glory; that your faith and hope might be in God. (1 Peter 1:18–21)

The anointing of God is very costly. Money can buy a whole lot of things; in fact, Solomon said in Ecclesiastes 10:19: "A feast is made for laughter, and wine makes merry: but money answers all things." Money might be the answer to the things pertaining to natural necessities. Oh, but it comes down to the things that the devil throws upon us, it is going to take the anointing of God to destroy the yoke. Our warfare is not with things that we can see or touch, but with things that are not seen or cannot be touched. Apostle Paul said in Ephesians 6:12: "For we wrestle not against flesh and blood, but against principalities, against powers, against the rulers of the darkness of this world, against spiritual wickedness in high places."

Now that I know what I am fighting against, I need this costly anointing for my warfare. I know that I am in a spiritual warfare, I have got to have a spiritual weapon. Apostle said in 2 Corinthians 10:3–5:

> For though we walk in the flesh, we do not war after the flesh. For the weapons of our warfare are not carnal, but mighty through God to the pulling down of strong holds. Casting down imaginations, and every high thing that exalts itself against the knowledge of God, and bringing into the captivity every thought to the obedience of Christ.

You know that the Bible tells us a whole lot about curses. Malachi said that our robbing God has caused this whole nation to be cursed with a curse. When God spoke through Malachi, the people turned and asked God, "How have we robbed you?" God answered and said, "In tithe and offerings."

Sometimes we bring ourselves under and into curses, and it is done out of ignorance. There was a time in the life of Apostle Paul when he acknowledged that he done a lot of wrong and cruel things, but he found favor with God because he done those things out of ignorance. Paul said this in 1 Timothy 1:12–13: "And I thank Christ Jesus our Lord, who hath enabled me, for that he counted me faithful, putting me in the ministry. Who was before a blasphemer, and persecutor, and injurious: but I obtained mercy because I did it ignorantly in unbelief."

THE GREAT TRIBULATION

As I have said, sometimes we obtain curses from doing things ignorantly, but the Lamb of God, he done nothing out of ignorance. There was no ignorance in him, but he made himself a curse to redeem us from the curse of the law. The Bible said in Galatians 3:13: "Christ hat redeemed us from the curse of the law, being made a curse for us: for it is written, cursed is everyone that hangs on a tree."

Back in the old books of the Bible and in the times of the laws, the Bible said in Deuteronomy 21:22–23:

> And if a man has committed a sin worthy of death, and he is put to death, and thou hang him on a tree: his body shall not remain all night upon the tree, but thou shalt in any wise bury him that day; (for he that is hanged is cursed of God) that thy land be not defiled, which the Lord thy God giveth thee for an inheritance.

That was why the world thought that God had put a curse upon his only begotten Son, not knowing that it was already foreordained by God to make his Son's soul an offering for our sins. The Bible said in Isaiah 53:10: "Yet it please the Lord to bruise him; he hath put him to grief: when thou shalt make his soul an offering for sin, he shall see his seed, he shall prolong his days, and the pleasure of the Lord shall prosper in his hand."

The Lamb of God was wounded, and he was bruised; not only was he wounded and bruised outwardly, but he was wounded and bruised inwardly as well. Sometimes, inward wounds and bruises are worse that the outward ones. Sometimes, the doctor will stich an open wound back together and give some medication for pain, and in a matter of time, it goes away. The bruises, sometimes we can rub them with alcohol, an ointment, or put a cold pack on them; and the pain is soothed. In time, and time's continuation, we look; and there is not a scar or mark of evidence that we have ever been bruised. Oh, but the inward wounds and bruises can and will last a lifetime or cause people to give up on life or living because they could not take the pain. Some people commit suicide because their hearts and minds could not deal with the oppression.

Well, the prophet Isaiah prophesied about the forth coming of the Lamb of God, and some of the ways that he would suffer before he would be slain. The Bible said, "He was oppressed, and he was afflicted, yet he opened not his mouth" (Isaiah 53:7).

The time was about to come in the life of Jesus that he was headed toward the end of his journey (the costly anointing), which the prophet Isaiah talked about when said, "He was taken from prison and from judgment: and who shall declare his generation? For he was cut off out of the land of the living for the transgressions of my people was he stricken" (Isaiah 58:8).

Jesus knew that he was headed toward finishing the works that his Father had sent him to do, and that the greater sufferings were about to begin, so he got his twelve disciples and sit down with them. The Bible said in Luke 22:14–15: "And when the hour was come, he set down and the twelve with him. And he said unto them, With desire, I have desired to eat this Passover with you before I suffer."

The eating of the Passover, it was the bread and the cup, which was the fruit of the vine. The bread represented the body of the Lamb of God. That was the last supper or Passover that Jesus had with his disciples. He told his disciples in Luke 22:16–18: "For I say unto you, I will not anymore eat thereof, until it be fulfilled in the kingdom of God. And he took the cup and gave thanks, and said, Take this and divide it among yourselves. For I say unto you, I will not drink of the fruit of the vine, until the kingdom of God shall come."

Jesus told his disciples and was telling the whole world that the bread was his body, and the cup, the fruit of the vine, would represent the shedding of his blood, which would be done for them and the whole world. We read this in the Bible: And he took bread and gave thanks and broke it, and gave unto them saying, this is my body which is given for you: do this in remembrance of me. Likewise, also the cup after supper saying, "This cup is the New Testament in my blood, which is shed for you" (Luke 22:19–20).

The Lamb of God was oppressed, was wounded, and was bruised; and as I had said earlier, some of the greatest wounds and

THE GREAT TRIBULATION

bruises are inward. I know that it had to be oppressing with the wounds and bruises upon Jesus's heart when had chosen those men to be his disciples. Many times, when he went to pray, they were with him. He blessed and broke bread, and they ate together.

In their breaking bread and eating, and drinking together, he had to tell them that one of them was a devil, and that he was going to betray him, and he let Judas know that he was that disciple. One day, Jesus had his disciple together, and he was talking to them. He knew that they had been out and among the people of the world and heard them talk about him, so he asked them, "Whom do the people say that I am?" Their Response were "Some say that you are John the Baptist, some say that you are Elijah, and others say that you are Jeremiah or one of the prophets." After Jesus had found out who the people thought he was, he wanted to know if his disciples really knew who he was. So he asked them, "Whom do you say that I am?" Simon Peter was the one who knew exactly who he was. The Bible said, "And Simon Peter answered and said, Thou art the Christ, the Son of the living God" (Matthew 16:16). Because of the fact that Simon Peter knew who Jesus was, he obtained keys to the kingdom and power to bind and to lose. In other words, powers were given unto him over all powers of the devil. The Bible continues,

> And Jesus answered and said unto him, Blessed art thou, Simon Bar-Jona: for flesh and blood hath not revealed it unto thee, but my Father which is in heaven. And I say unto thee, That thou art Peter, and upon this rock I will build my church; and the gates of hell shall not prevail against it. And I will give unto thee the keys of the kingdom of heaven: and whatsoever thou shalt bind on earth shall be bound in heaven: and whatsoever thou shalt loose on earth shall be loosed in heaven. (Matthew 16:17–19)

Jesus loved Peter so much after he had given Peter the keys to the kingdom to bind the works of the devil, and to lose and set the captive free, Jesus knew that the devil wanted to destroy Peter, the costly anointing, so he prayed that Peter would have a faith that would not fail him. Jesus told Peter, "The Lord said, Simon, Simon, behold, Satan hath desired to have you, (the costly anointing) that he may sift you as wheat: But I have prayed for thee, that thy faith fails not: and when thou art converted, strengthen thy brethren" (Luke 22:31–32).

It is amazing how we can move by the power of God, and as Paul said, "Nay, in all these things, we are more than conquers through him that loved us" (Romans 8:37). In talking about the Lord, Jesus Christ, the Lamb of God, Peter was in a place that he thought that he was equal with Jesus. He thought that he could suffer through and that he would be able to die the same type of death that Jesus was going to die. That was because Jesus had given him the keys to the kingdom, the anointing to bind and to lose.

I can imagine Jesus looking at Peter and saying,

> "Boy, you are not ready for this as you suppose. You do not know me like you think you do. I am going to fall into the hands of sinners, and they are going to do some stuff unto me, and you are going to be standing and watching, and when they shall ask you, "Peter, do you know this man Jesus?" You are going to deny the fact that you have ever know me. You will start cussing and swearing that you do not even know me. By then, Peter said, "Lord, I'm ready to go with thee both into prison and death." Jesus told Peter, "I tell thee, Peter, the cock shall not crow this day before thou shall thrice deny that thou know me. (Luke 22:33–34)

Talking about oppressions, Jesus had a disciple, Judas, who betrayed him and turned him over into the hands of sinners for them to kill him. I can understand why the Bible said that the love of money is the root of all evil. Judas loved money, and he was ready

THE GREAT TRIBULATION

to sell Jesus out for only a few pieces of silver. We read this in the Bible: "The one of the twelve called Judas Iscariot, went into the chief priests; and he said unto them, What will you give me, and I will deliver him unto you? And they covenant with him for thirty pieces of silver. And from that time, he sought opportunity to betray him" (Matthew 26:14–16).

The Bible said that after Jesus and his disciples had communed and broke bread and ate and drank of the cup, the fruit of the vine for the last time here on earth; they went out into the Mount of Olives. But before they had left, they sang a hymn. The Bible does not tell what hymn they sang, but the Bible does tell us that Jesus is a friend that sticks closer than a brother. To me, the appropriate hymn would have been, "What a friend we have in Jesus, all our sins and griefs he bears, what a privilege to carry everything to him in prayer. Have we trials and temptations? Is there troubles anywhere? O what needless pain we bear, all because we do not carry everything to him in prayer."

The prophet Isaiah said, "Surely he has borne our griefs and carried our sorrows," and that is why the writer of Hebrews said, "For we have not a high priest which cannot be touch with the feelings of our infirmities; but was in all points tempted like as we are, yet without sin." As the words in the hymn said, "What a privilege to carry everything to him in prayer." Well, Hebrews 4:16 said, "Let us therefore come boldly to the throne of grace, that we may obtain mercy, and find grace to help in time of need."

"The anointed one, he was acquainted with grief, and was a man of sorrows."

His griefs and sorrows are written in Isaiah 53:3–5:

> He was despised and rejected of men; a man of sorrows, and acquainted with grief; and we hid as it were our faces from him; he was despised, and we esteemed him not. Surely, he hath borne our griefs, and carried our sorrows; yet we did esteem him stricken, and smitten of God, and afflicted. But he was wounded for our transgres-

sions, he was bruised for our iniquities: the chastisement of our peace was upon him; and with his stripes we are healed.

The times of Jesus's griefs and sorrows were at hand, and he knew that it was time to pray. He prayed to bear my griefs and to carry my sorrows; that is why he told me in Matthew 11:28–30, "Come unto me all ye that labor and are heavy laden, and I will give you rest. Take my yoke upon you and learn of me; for I am meek and lowly in heart; and ye shall find rest unto your souls. For my yoke is easy and my burden is light."

Jesus said that his yoke is easy, and his burden is light. My grief, my pain, and my sorrows are not identical to those of Jesus. He has already borne and carried them for me. I got to do what he told me in 1 Peter 5:7: "Casting all your care upon him; for he cares for you." I cannot take any matters into my own hands no matter how great or small it seems to be. I got to do what is said in Philippians 4:6, "Be careful for nothing: but in everything by prayer and supplication and with thanksgiving, let your request be made know unto God."

When I have done these things, he continues to say in Philippians 4:7, "And the peace of God which passes all understanding, shall keep your heart and minds through Christ Jesus."

Jesus went to a place called Gethsemane to pray. He took some of his disciples with him, Peter and the two sons of Zebedee, and the Bible said that he began to be sorrowful and very heavy. The Bible said that he said unto them, "My soul is exceeding sorrowful, even unto death; tarry ye here, and watch with me" (Matthew 26:38). Jesus was at the point and time in his life wherein he felt the inward pains, burdens, and sorrows in his fleshly body.

Peter said that when we have suffered in the flesh, then we will cease from sin. Well, Jesus did not have any sins that he needed to cease from, but he gave himself as a ransom for all to be justified in due time.

With Jesus, the burdens became heavier and the pains more severe, so we read this in the Bible: "And he went a little farther, and he fell on his face, and prayed, saying, O my Father, if it be possible,

THE GREAT TRIBULATION

let this cup pass from me: nevertheless, not as I will, but as thou wilt" (Matthew 26:39).

Now, Peter had told Jesus, "Lord I am ready to go with you both into prison and to death." But when Jesus was praying, Peter could not stay awake. And when Jesus found him asleep, he said, "What, could you not watch with me one hour?" (Matthew 26:40). Jesus talked to Peter about the weakness of the flesh and what to do so that he would not enter temptation: "Watch and pray, that ye enter not into temptation; the spirit indeed is willing, but the flesh is weak" (Matthew 26:41). No matter how painful it became with Jesus, there was always a prayer prayed unto his father for his will to be done. No matter how bitter the cup became, he was willing to drink of it. He prayed, "O my Father, if this cup may not pass away from me, except I drink of it, thy will be done" (Mathew 26:42).

I wonder, how in the world could those disciples sleep in such a time as it was when their savior was in agony, suffering, and was about to go to prison for a crime that he did not commit and to pay a debt that he did not owe. Jesus was on his way to prison and death, and Peter was yet sleeping. The Bible said, "And he came and found them asleep again: for their eyes were heavy" (Matthew 26:43). Jesus left them a third time and went and prayed the same prayer, and he came back unto them, and he told them that they could sleep on and take their rest, for it was time for him to be betrayed. In Matthew 26:45, we read, "Then comes he to his disciples, and said unto them, Sleep on now, and take your rest; behold, the hour is at hand, and the son of man is betrayed into the hands of sinners."

I wonder if Judas realized that Jesus was suffering and dying for the sins of the whole world, which would have included him. Jesus talked about how he was laying down his life for his friends and that he would no longer call them servants but friends. The Bible said,

> Greater love hath no man than this, that a man lay down his life for his friends. Ye are my friends, if you do whatsoever I command you. Henceforth, I call you not servants; for the servant knows not what his lord doeth; but I have

called you friends; for all things that I have heard of my Father I have made known unto you. (John 15:13–15)

So when Judas came to betray Jesus with a kiss, he called him "friend" because he knew what his master had done and was doing. He was always right there, even when Jesus went into the garden to pray. When he betrayed Jesus, he knew exactly where to go. The Bible said in John 18:2, "And Judas also, which betrayed him knew the place, for Jesus often resorted thither with his disciples." When Judas came to Jesus and said, "Hail, master," and kissed him; Jesus said unto him, "Friend, wherefore art thou come?? Them cam they and laid hand on Jesus, and took him" (Matthew 26:50).

"The crying in pain, I can explain, the costly anointing has been my gain."

Most of my life, I felt like no one loved me or cared about what happened to me. At the age of nineteen, I was contemplating suicide. I felt that nobody cared and that nobody would miss me. But a little bit better than five years later, I heard about a man whose name was Jesus. He gave an invitation when he said, "Come unto me all ye that labor and are heavy laden, and I will give you rest" (Matthew 11:28). The host of heaven knew that I need some peace, which the Bible sometimes relates peace and rest as being the same thing. On February 4, 1970, I had been raped, and at that time, I was a virgin. My suspected pregnancy was my reason for contemplating suicide, but glory be unto God, he had a purpose for me to live.

I cried and I cried, and so many times I asked the Lord, "Why me, Lord? Why did you let this happen to me when you knew that I was a virgin, and that I wanted to be a virgin until the day that I got married? Lord, you knew the intentions I had for my life." I had intentions, but God had a plan, and his was greater and far better than mine. God knew better than me what I was capable of handling, what I could endure and go through.

From the time that I was raped, I went through twenty-five years of crying in pain and sometimes feeling like I was going to lose my mind, not knowing that the same thing had happened to so

THE GREAT TRIBULATION

many people. Some did lose their minds, some did kill themselves, and some turned to homosexuality; but God chose me to be victimized in that manner to put an anointing upon my life that would destroy the yoke off the lives of others.

I cannot give the number of children, women, and men that God has revealed and spoken prophetically unto them as to what had happened in their lives; and God anointed me to lay hands and to bind and to lose and to cause them who were held captive inwardly to be made free. Not everything had been done or spoken prophetically, but there were many people that had heard my overcoming testimony, and voluntarily, they told me what had happen to them and how they fell victim. When they talked to me, I knew that was a cry for help. God suffered me to be victimized and made me an overcomer so that in his name, I could be a deliverer.

I have had people to come and tell me, "My father is the father of my child. My mother knew that my father was doing this unto me, and she didn't stand for me. She didn't try to protect me." Someone told me, "My mother's boyfriend fathered my baby, but my mother let him continue to live in the house with us." I have had men to tell me, "When I was a little boy, my uncles molested me. A friend of the family molested me." A young man once said to me, "My sister had to go to prison because she molested me." I could go on and on talking about the victims, but today, all those victims have become victors. With this type of deliverance, or maybe I should say, with this type anointing, it is priceless. It is called the costly anointing.

When my husband told me that he did not want me anymore, and that the next time that I would see him, he would be with a real woman, that really caused my heart to hurt. I loved that man so much until I thought that my life could not go on without him. But when Jesus came into my life, I discovered that he was the man that I could not live without.

It hurt me so deeply when I would see him with his other wife (bigamist), the one that took my place. I was saved, so I would pray, "Lord, please bring my husband back to me and my children." I relied on the scripture that said, "And this confidence that we have in him, that if we ask anything according to his will, he hears us" (1

John 5:14). I just knew that this was the will of God because this was the man to whom I was married. I am in the hand of God, and I trust him with all my heart; and when I was crying in pain because my heart was so burden, I remembered, all that was in God's divine will. God has taken my life to use as an example, that through Christ Jesus, I can triumph and overcome anything and all things because greater is Christ Jesus who is in me than he that is in the world—none other than that old serpent the devil.

Men would come around and flash money in my face, and God knows that in those times, I needed it because I did not have food in the house to feed my children. However, I trusted and believed God. I would tell those men, "Take your money home to your wife," and sometimes they would say, "I don't have a wife," then I would tell them, "Take it to your woman." I would not even give them the time of the day because I was totally committed to God.

God did not want me to have a husband because he wanted me to have the testimony that God would be that husband, and that God would be that father and the provider for my children. My children never went hungry; in fact, they never knew that there was no food in the house until June 2016, when they read my book *I Overcame by the Blood of the Lamb*. In fact, they were amazed and hurt when they read about some of the things I had gone through in life.

God proved himself unto me when he said, "Let me be your husband. I will love you unconditionally with an everlasting love. I will never leave you, nor will I forsake you. I will be with you always, even until the end of the world." Jesus said in John 15:13, "Greater love hath no man than this: that a man lay down his life for his friends." When Jesus was hanging on the cross before he died, he bore my sin in his body. He bore my griefs and he carried my sorrows, and that is what has caused my yoke to be easy and my burdens to be light.

Jesus is the anointed one. He was the anointed one before he came down from heaven and entered a fleshly body that his Father had prepared for him. His suffering in a fleshly body was an example for us, and it is said in 1 Peter 4:1, "For as much then, as Christ has suffered for us in the flesh, arm yourselves likewise with the same

THE GREAT TRIBULATION

mind; for he that hath suffered in the flesh hath ceased from sin." I have learned that there is nothing that I go through that Jesus had not gone through already. That is why he said In Hebrews 4:15, "For we have not a high priest which cannot be touched with the feelings of our infirmities, but was in all points tempted as we are, yet without sin."

I went through most of life being alone and feeling like nobody loved me or cared about me, which was the type of life that Jesus lived. His own people did not receive him as we read in John 1:11: "He came unto his own, and his own receive him not." There were times when I thought that Jesus's disciples really, really loved him, especially when he told them, "I am not going to call you servants, but I am going to call you friends because a servant doesn't know what his master does, but you know what I do and where I go." Well, I learned differently about their love for Jesus. Jesus told Peter, "Before the cock crow, thou shalt deny me thrice." When Jesus told Peter that, Peter and the other disciples said in Matthew 26:35: "Peter said unto him, 'Though I should die with thee, yet will I not deny thee: likewise said all the disciples.'" True love comes from the heart, and love will not let you run off when a friend is in trouble.

"At Jesus's betrayal and arrest, that is what happened: They ran off."

In the same hour, said Jesus to the multitude, "Are you come out against a thief, with swords and staves for to take me? I sat daily with you teaching in the temple, and you laid no hold on me. But all this was done that the scriptures of the prophet might be fulfilled. Then all the disciples forsook him and fled" (Matthew 26:55–56).

Jesus lives in me, and that makes me to be a Son of God, as is illustrated in 1 John 2:3: "Beloved, now ye are the Sons of God, and it doth not ye appear what we should be; but we know that when he shall appear, we shall be like him: for we shall see him as he is." In other words, the word of God has told me that I am going to see Jesus as he is because I am going to be just like him; I got to suffer even as he suffered. I got to be persecuted. I am going to be hated. I am going to be rejected. I am going to be falsely accused and abused;

some of all those things have happened in my life. And as I yet live, there will be more things that I must suffer through.

I really, really give honor and glory to my Lord and Savior Jesus Christ who has caused me to triumph and overcome. This is very costly. He took me with all my flaws and took all my insecurities away and put his word in me, "I want you to go and preach my gospel." This is the costly anointing.

After I began to preach the gospel, Jesus told me, "I am giving unto you a prophetic ministry." In this ministry, he has entrusted me with the deep secrets of God. In this ministry, he has spoken life and has given life when death was knocking at the doors. In this ministry, he has caused drug addicts to become addicted to the ministry and to the word of the Lord. This is the costly anointing.

Thanks to you, Jesus, for being with me in the most difficult times of my life. When it seemed and looked like all hope was gone, your word was fulfilled when you told me, "I will never leave you nor will I forsake you. I will be with you always even until the end of the world." Jesus, I thank you for choosing me to suffer and to go through what I went through. It is a fact that I was never alone. You were always with me. From these things and with these things, I obtained something that is priceless, it is the costly anointing. Glory be unto the Lamb of God.

"It is going to take the costly anointing to be a chosen vessel for the great tribulation and to be able to stand."

Chapter 5

The Great Tribulation

The word *tribulation* has a whole lot of definitions. Some synonyms for tribulations that the saints shall encounter are adversity, sufferings, distress, persecutions, sorrows, burdens, and many, many more. Tribulations come when one is confined in a narrow place. Jesus loves us so much that not any of these things can come between his love and us. The Bible said,

> Who is he that condemns? It is Christ that died, yea rather, that is risen again, who is even at the right hand of God, who also makes intercession for us. Who shall separate us from the love of Christ? Shall tribulation or distress, or persecution, or famine, or nakedness, or peril, or sword? As it is written, For thy sake, we are killed all the day long; we are accounted as sheep for the slaughter. Nay, in all these things we are more than conquerors through him that loved us. For I am persuaded, that neither death, nor life, nor angels, nor principalities, nor powers, nor things present, nor things to come. Nor height, nor depth, nor any other creature, shall be able to separate us from the love of God, which is in Christ Jesus our Lord. (Romans 8:34–39)

PASTOR CHRISTINE PEEBLES

Jesus does not want us to be caught up or carried away by the things of this world and the cares of this life; for when the great tribulations shall come, none of these things shall save or protect us. Paul said in Colossians 3:1–3, "IF ye then be risen with Christ, seek those things which are above, where Christ sit on the right hand of God. Set your affections on things above, and not on the things on earth. For ye are dead, and your life is hidden with Christ in God."

"Woe be unto the hypocrites."

In this generation, there is a whole lot of hypocrisy coming forth in the church. The meaning of hypocrisy is failure to practice what you preach. Jesus warns us to not follow the Scribes and the Pharisees because they speak one thing, and they do something else. The Bible said, "THEN SPOKE Jesus to the multitude and his disciples. Saying, The Scribes and the Pharisees sit in Moses' seat: All therefore, whatsoever they bid you observe, that observe and do, but do not ye after their works: for they say and do not" (Matthew 23:1–3).

Church folk are now doing things for an outside show to the world, or to make a name for themselves. Paul said 1 Corinthians 10:31: "Whether therefore ye eat or drink, or whatsoever you do, do it all to the glory of God." God gives warnings and woes to the people who are hypocritical, wanting to be seen and heard. The Bible said,

> Woe unto you, Scribes, and Pharisees, and hypocrites! For ye pay tithe a mint and anise and cumin, and have omitted the weightier matters of the law, judgment, mercy, and faith: these ought ye to have done, and not to leave the other undone. Ye blind guides, which strain at a gnat, and swallow a camel. Woe unto ye Scribes, Pharisees, and hypocrites! For ye make clean the outside of the cup, and of the platter, but within they are full of extortion and excess. Thou blind Pharisees, cleanse first that which is within the cup and the platter, that the outside of them may be clean also. Woe unto you Scribes, Pharisees, and hypocrites! For ye are like unto

THE GREAT TRIBULATION

> whited sepulchres which indeed appear beautiful outward, but are within full of dead men bones, and of all uncleanness. Even so ye also outwardly appear righteous unto men, but within ye are full of hypocrisy and iniquity. Woe unto ye Scribes and Pharisees, and hypocrites! Because ye build the tombs of the prophets, and garnish the sepulchres of the righteous. And say, If we had been in the days of our fathers, we would not have been partakers with them in the blood of the prophets. Wherefore ye be witnesses unto yourselves, that ye are the children of them which killed the prophets. Fill ye up then the measure of your fathers. Ye serpents, ye generation of vipers, how can ye escape the damnation of hell? (Matthew 23:23–33)

God is yet saying, "Woe! Woe! Woe! He is sending forth his wrath and his judgment, but not like it is going to come forth." Before the coming of the Lord Jesus Christ, there is going to be a falling away from him, and then the man of sin, the son of perdition shall be revealed. The Bible said,

> Now we beseech you, brethren, by the coming of our Lord Jesus Christ, and by our gathering together unto him. That ye be not soon shaken in mind, or be troubled, neither by spirit, nor by word, nor by letter as from us, as that the day of Christ is at hand. Le no man, deceive you by any means: for that day shall not come, except there come a falling away first, and that man of sin be revealed, the son of perdition. Who opposes and exalts himself above all that is called God, or that is worshipped; so that he as God sits in the temple of God, showing himself that he is God. Remember ye not that. When I was yet with you,

PASTOR CHRISTINE PEEBLES

I told you these things. And you know what with-holds that he might be revealed in his time. For the mystery of iniquity doth already work: only he who now let's will let, until he be taken out of the way. And then shall that wicked be revealed, whom the Lord shall consume with the spirit of his mouth, and shall destroy with the brightness of his coming. Even him whose coming is after the working of Satan with all powers and signs and lying wonders. And with all deceivableness of unrighteousness in them that perish; because they received not the love of the truth, that they might be saved. And for this cause God shall send them strong delusion, and they should believe a lie. That they all might be damned who believed not the truth, but had pleasure in unrighteous-ness. (2 Thessalonians 2:1–12)

"The coming of the Son of man shall be liken unto the days of Noah and the days of Lot."

When the first world was destroyed by the flood, God had a rem-nant; he had a remnant when he destroyed Sodom and Gomorrah. God does not let destruction come before warnings. He said in Proverbs 16:18: "Pride goes before destruction, and a haughty spirit before a fall. God had a righteous man, Noah to gather some people, seven and himself, and the creatures into the ark; those were who and what he was going to save." The Bible said,

AND THE LORD said unto Noah, Come, thou and all thou house into the ark; for thee have I seen righteous before me in this genera-tion. Of every clean beast thou shalt take to thee by sevens, the male, and his female; and of beasts that are not clean by two, the male and his female. Of the fowls of the air by sevens, the male, and the female, to keep seed alive upon the earth. For

THE GREAT TRIBULATION

yet seven days, and I will cause it to rain upon the earth forty days and forty nights; and every living substance that I have made will I destroy from the face of the earth. And Noah did according unto all that the Lord commanded him. And Noah was six hundred years old when the flood of water was upon the earth. And Noah went in, and his sons, and his wife, and his son's wives with him, into the ark, because of the waters of the flood. Of clean bests, and of beasts that are not clean, and of fowls, and of everything that creeps upon the earth. There went in two and two unto Noah into the ark, the male, and the female, as God had commanded Noah. And it came to pass after seven days, that the waters of the flood were upon the earth. In the six hundredth year of Noah's life, in the second month, the seventeenth day of the month, the same day were the fountains of the great deep broken up, and the windows of heaven were opened. And the rain was upon the earth forty days and forty nights. In the selfsame day entered Noah, and Shem, and Ham, and Japheth, the sons of Noah, and Noah's wife, and the three wives of his sons with them, into the ark. (Genesis 7:1–13)

In the days of Lot, he had a wife, two daughters, and two sons-in-law; they all lived in the city that God was getting ready to destroy because of the wickedness. Lot's sons-in-law were as the people are today; they rather to enjoy the pleasures of sin, which is only for a season. Lot did not want his sons-in-law to be destroyed, but when he spoke to them about leaving the city, they made a mockery of it. The Bible said,

For we will destroy this place, because the cry of them were waxen great before the face of

PASTOR CHRISTINE PEEBLES

> the Lord; and the Lord hath sent us to destroy it. And Lot went out, and spoke unto his sons in law, which married his daughters, and said, "Up, get you out of this place, for the Lord will destroy this city. But he seemed as one that mocked unto his sons in law." (Genesis 19:13–14)

When the Lord brings us out of something, he would have us to not look back, but go forward and have a press within us. Paul said in Philippians 3:13–14: "Brethren, I count not myself to have apprehended; but this one thing that I do, forgetting those things which are behind, and reaching forth unto those things which are before me." I press toward the mark of the prize of the high calling of God in Christ Jesus. God delivered Lot and his family out of Sosom and Gomorrah before he destroyed the cities. When God said do not look back, he meant not to look back. The sins of whatever, it will destroy us if it is not delivered out of our hearts. Lot's wife did not turn loose those cities in her heart, so her end was turning into a pillar of salt. The Bible said,

> And when the morning arose, then the angels hastened Lot, saying, "Arise, take thy wife, and thy two daughters, which are here; lest thou be consumed in the iniquity of the city. And while he lingered, the men laid hold upon the hand of his wife, and upon the hand of his two daughters; the Lord being merciful unto him: and they brought him forth, and set him without the city. And it came to pass, when they had brought them forth abroad, that he said, Escape for thy life; look not behind thee, neither stay thou in all the plain; escape to the mountain, lest thou be consumed. And Lot said unto them, Oh, not so, my Lord. And he said unto him, See, I have accepted thee concerning this thing also, that I will not overthrow this city for the which thy hast

THE GREAT TRIBULATION

spoken. Haste thee, escape thither, for I cannot do anything till thou be come thither. Therefore, the name of the city was called Zoar. The sun was risen upon the earth when Lot entered Zoar. Then the Lord rained upon Sodom and upon Gomorrah brimstone and fire from the Lord out of heaven. And he overthrew those cities, and all the plain, and all the inhabitants of the cities, and that which grew upon the ground. But his wife looked back from behind him, and she became a pillar of salt. (Genesis 19:15–18, 21–26)

"Souls that were saved in the days of Noah, and in the days of Lot."

Jesus suffered for sins and was put to death in the flesh; afterward, he went down into hell and preached to the souls that were disobedient when Noah was preparing the ark. The remnant doing the days of Noah consisted of eight souls. The Bible said,

> For Christ also hath once suffered for sins, the just for the unjust, that he might bring us to God, being put to death in the flesh, but quickened by the Spirit. By the which also he went and preached unto the spirits in prison. Which sometime were disobedient, when the longsuffering of God waited in the days of Noah, while the ark was a preparing, wherein few, that is, eight souls were saved by water. (1 Peter 3:18–20)

God did not tolerate sin from the angels; he casted them down into hell. God did not tolerate sin from the old world; only the preacher and seven more people were saved. When God turned the cities of Sodom and Gomorrah into ashes, the Bible said that he delivered just Lot. God did not spare them, and he is not going to spare this generation. The Bible said,

PASTOR CHRISTINE PEEBLES

For if God spared not the angels that sinned, but cast them into hell, and delivered them into chains of darkness, to be reserved unto judgment. And spared not the old world, but saved Noah the eight person a preacher of righteousness, bringing in the flood upon the world of the ungodly. And delivered just Lot, vexed with the filthy conversation of the wicked. (For the righteous man dwelling among them, in seeing and hearing, vexed his righteous soul from day to day with their unlawful deeds). The Lord knows how to deliver the godly out of temptations, and reserve the unjust unto the day of judgment to be punished. (2 Peter 2:4–9)

The Bible tells us that as it was in the days of Noah and in the days of Lot, so shall it be also in the days of the Son of man. The Bible tells us what the world was doing in those days. The Bible said,

And as it was in the days of Noe, so shall it be also in the days of the Son of man. They did eat, they drank, they married wives, they were given in marriage, until the day that Noe entered the ark, and the flood came, and destroyed them all. Likewise, also as it was in the days of Lot; they did eat, they drank, they bought, they sold, they planted, they build; but the same day that Lot went out of Sodom it rained fire and brimstone from heaven, and destroyed them all. Even thus shall it be in the day when the Son of man is revealed. Jesus is telling us, "Get it right now, do not wait until we see these things coming, and try to turn back or try to turn things around. He reminds us to remember what happened to Lot's wife.

THE GREAT TRIBULATION

The Bible went on to say,

> In that day, he which shall be upon the housetop, and his stuff in the house, let him not come down to take to take it away: and he that is in the field, let him likewise not return back. Remember Lot's wife. Whosoever shall seek to save his life shall lose it, and whosoever shall lose his life shell preserve it. (Matthew 17:26–33)

"The days of Noah, the days of Lot, the days of the Son of man."

The Bible said that in the days of Noah, they ate, they drink, they married wives, and they were giving in marriage. They did all those things and some more until the day that Noah entered in the ark, and the flood came and destroyed them all. The Bible said that in the days of Lot, they did eat, they drank, they bought and sold, they planted, and they build. But the same day that Lot went out of Sodom, it rained fire and brimstone from heaven and destroyed them all. The Bible said that it is going to be the same when the Son of man is revealed.

Well, the time has come when the Son of man is being revealed. They ate, they drank; that is what the church is doing now. About everything that the church does pertaining to prayer, it revolves around eating and drinking. The church is having prayer breakfasts, praying, and eating. The folk bellies are filled with food and drinks, and demonic spirits are taking over and controlling the minds of people. Demons are cast out through by fasting and praying. In the Bible, a man brought his lunatic son unto Jesus's disciples as they could not cast the demons out, and they wanted to know why. Jesus told them, "This kind goes out only by fasting and praying." The Bible said,

> And when they were come to the multitude, there came to him a certain man, kneeling down to him, and saying, Lord have mercy

PASTOR CHRISTINE PEEBLES

> on my son: for he is a lunatic, and sore vexed: for oftentimes he falls into the fire, and often into the water. And I brought him to thy disciples, and they could not cure him. Then Jesus answered and said, O faithless and perverse generation, how long shall I be with you? How long shall I suffer you? Bring him hither to me. And Jesus rebuked the devil; and the child was cured from thar very hour. Then came the disciples to Jesus apart, and said, Why could not we cast him out? And Jesus said unto them, Because of your unbelief: for verily I say unto you, if ye have faith as a grain of mustard seed, ye shall say unto this mountain, Remove hence to yonder place; and it shall remove; and nothing shall be impossible unto you. Howbeit this kind goes not out but by prayer and fasting. (Matthew 17:14–21)

People, church folk, they are not understanding that church is not a building, but it is the body of Christ. The Bible said in Ephesians 1:22–23, "And hath put all things under his feet, and gave him to be the head over all things to the church. Which is his body, the fulness of him that fills all in all." Talking about the birth of the church, before Jesus went back to heaven, he instructed his disciples what to do, where to go, and what they should do for the church to be birthed. The Bible said, "And, behold, I send the promise of my Father upon you: but tarry ye in the city of Jerusalem, until ye be endued with power from on high" (Luke 24:49).

The day that the church was first birth was called the day of Pentecost. The Bible said,

> AND WHEN the day of Pentecost was fully come, they were all with one accord in one place. And suddenly there came a sound from heaven as of a rushing mighty wind, and it filled all the house where they were sitting. And there

THE GREAT TRIBULATION

> appeared unto them cloven tongues like as of fire, and it sat upon each of them. And they were all filled with the Holy Ghost, and began to speak with other tongues, as the Spirit gave them utterance. (Acts 2:1–4)

If the church is not birth forth, then she shall have no power. People have put the mule before the cart; they are trying to have Holy Ghost power before the Holy Ghost comes. The power comes after the Holy Ghost. The Bible said, "But ye shall receive power after that the Holy Ghost is come upon you: and you shall be witnesses unto me both in Jerusalem, and in all Judaea, and in Samaria, and unto the uttermost part of the earth" (Acts 1:8). Birth coming forth is not something that is going to happen overnight; we have got to wait. The Bible said on the day of Pentecost, they tarried. In tarrying, which means waiting, there is got to be some crying, weeping, and mourning, and travailing. We cannot expect birth to come forth in a day or all at once; we have got to wait in prayer. The prophet Isaiah said, "Who hath heard such a thing? Who hath seen such a thing? Shall the earth be made to bring forth in one day? Or shall a nation be born at once? For as soon as Zion travailed, she brought forth her children" (Isaiah 66:8).

In the days of Noah and in the days of Lot, they were marrying and giving in marriage; those are the things that are happening now. Men and women are doing marriages as they do an old pair of shoes, lots of times, new shoes: "These are old" or "I do not like these anymore. I am going to throw these away and get me some new ones." Apostles, pastors, evangelists, bishops, and so on, some of them have two, three, four, five and so on, living wives and living husbands, and do not see anything wrong with that; and the congregation is following right along in their footsteps. God is raising up some preachers who are going to cry loud and spare not. God is going to raise up some preachers that will preach repentance as John the Baptist preach, letting people know that it is wrong to have someone else husband or wife. John knew that he had to preach those things even if it caused him his life, and it did. The Bible said, "And Herod himself had sent forth and laid hold upon John, and bound him in prison for Herodias sake, his brother Philip's wife: for he had married her. For John had said unto Herod, it is not lawful for thee to have thy brother's wife" (Mark 6:17–18).

In the days of Noah and in the days of Lot, they bought, they sold, they planted, and they build; Jesus let the people know, and we are to know that life does not consist of the abundance of the things in which we possess. One day, we are going to die and leave it all and could be eternally lost. The Bible said,

> And he said unto them, Take heed, and beware of the covetousness; for a man's life consists not in the abundance of the things which he possesses. And he spoke a parable unto them saying, The ground of a certain rich man brought forth plentifully. And he thought within himself, saying, What shall I do, because I have no room where to bestow my fruits? And he said, This will I do: I will pull down my barns, and build greater; and there will I bestow my fruits and my goods. And I will say to my soul, Soul, thou hast much goods laid up for many years; take thine ease, eat, drink, and be merry. But God said unto him, Thou fool, this night thy soul shall be required of thee: then whose shall those things be, which thou hast provided? So is he that lays up treasures for himself, and is not rich toward God. And he said unto his disciples, Therefore I say unto you, Take no thought for your life, what ye shall eat, neither for the body, what ye shall put on. The life is more than meat, and the body is more than raiment. (Luke 12:15–23)

"The days of the Son of man."

The Bible spoke of the things that were being done before the days of destruction in the days of Noah and in the days of Lot. Now,

THE GREAT TRIBULATION

in the days of the Son of man, he had been in the temple teaching and giving woes to the Scribes, the Pharisees, and the hypocrites. He warned his disciples not to do as they had done. Jesus told them that they talked one thing, but they lived and did something else. Well, that is what is happening in the church today; the lives are not coinciding with the gospel that is being preached. That does not include everybody and all preachers, but when it comes down to the body, there is a majority. When John was on the isle of Patmos to get the word of God and the testimony of Jesus Christ, he was not instructed to send what he was hearing and seeing that was going on or that had happened to the world; John was told to write it in a book and send it to the churches. The Bible said, "Saying, I am Alpha and Omega, the first and the last: and what thou see, write in a book, and send it to the seven churches which are in Asia; unto Ephesus, and unto Smyrna, and unto Pergamos, and unto Thyatira, and unto Sardis, and unto Philadelphia, and unto Laodicea" (Revelation 1:11). My God, my God, the first church that John wrote to, the church of Ephesus, I can see that church in the now—the apostles that are liars, and Jesus, pleading with the church to return unto him. The Bible said,

> UNTO THE angel of the church of Ephesus write; These thing saith he that holds the seven stars in his right hand, who walks in the midst of the seven golden candlesticks. I know thy works, and thy labor, and thy patience, and how thou canst not bear them which are evil, and thou hast tried them which say they are apostles, and are not, and hast found them liars: And hast borne, and hast patience, and for my name's sake hast labored, and hast not fainted. Nevertheless, I have somewhat against thee, because thou hast left thy first love. Remember therefore from whence thou art fallen, and repent, and do the first works; or else I will come unto thee quickly, and will remove thy candlestick out of his place,

except thou repent. But this thou hast, that thou hate the deeds of the Nicolaitans, which I also hate. He that hath an ear, let him hear what the Spirit saith unto the churches: To him that overcomes will I give to eat of the tree of life, which is in the midst of the paradise of God. (Revelation 2:1–7)

Jesus's disciples came unto him when he came out of the temple to show him the buildings of the temple. They were devastated when Jesus told them what was going to happen to those buildings. They wanted to know when those things were going to happen, and what would be the sign of his coming, and when the world was going to end. The Bible said,

AND JESUS went out, and departed from the temple: and his disciples came to him for to show him the buildings of the temple. And Jesus said unto them, See ye not all these things? There shall not be left here one stone upon another, that shall not be thrown down. And as he sat upon the mount of olives, the disciples came unto privately, saying, Tell us, When shall these things be? And what shall be the sign of thy coming, and of the end of the world? (Matthew 24:1–3)

"Signs of the end of the age."

Jesus does not in anywise want us to be deceived; therefore, he warns us about those who are going to come in his name, and many are going to be deceived. He warns us about the things that are going to take place and what we shall see happening. He lets us know that when we shall see these things, we need to stand in the holy place. The world is already seeing some of the things that Jesus had spoken of. The Bible said,

THE GREAT TRIBULATION

> And Jesus answered and said unto them, Take heed that no man deceive you. For many shall come in my name, saying that I am Christ; and shall deceive many. And ye shall hear of wars and rumors of wars: see that ye be not troubled: for all these things must come to pass, but the end is not yet. For nation shall rise against nation, and kingdom against kingdom: and there shall be famines, and pestilences, and earthquakes in diver's places. All these are the beginning of sorrows. Then shall they deliver you up to be afflicted, and shall kill you: and ye shall be hated of all nations for my name's sake. And then shall many be offended, and shall betray one another, and shall hate one another. And many false prophets shall rise, and shall deceive many. And because iniquity shall abound, the love of many shall wax cold. But he that shall endue unto the end, the same shall be saved. And this gospel of the kingdom shall be preached in all the world for a witness unto all nations, and then shall the end come. When ye therefore shall see the abomination of desolation, spoken of by Daniel the prophet, stand in the holy place, (whoso reads, let him understand).

Speaking of the abominations and the desolation, Daniel saw where the Messiah was going to be cut off, but it was not going to be for himself. He saw where the overspreading of abominations, when consumed, that is what shall bring on desolation. The Bible said,

> And after threescore and two weeks shall Messiah be cut off, but not for himself: and the people of the prince that shall come shall destroy the city and the sanctuary; and the end shall be with a flood, and unto the end of the war des-

olations are determined. And he shall confirm the covenant with many for one week: and in the midst of the week, he shall cause the sacrifice and the oblation to cease, and for the overspreading of abominations he shall make it desolate, even until the consummation, and that determined shall be poured upon the desolate. (Daniel 9:26–27)

Abominations come forth through people who profess that they know Christ, but in their works, they deny him. Paul talked about that in the book of Titus 1:16: "They profess that they know God; but in works they deny him, being abominable, and disobedient, and unto every good work reprobate (void of judgment)." Concerning abominations, Paul also said in 2 Timothy 3:1–5:

THIS KNOW also, that in the last days perilous times shall come. For me shall be lovers of their own selves, covetous, boasters, proud, blasphemers, disobedient to parents, unthankful, unholy. Without natural affection, trucebreakers, false accusers, incontinent, fierce, despisers of those that are good. Traitors, heady, high minded, lovers of pleasures more than lovers of God. Having a form of godliness, but denying the powers thereof: from such turn away.

The abomination of desolation spoken of by Daniel the prophet is found in Matthew 24:15, Jesus said when we read that, get an understanding. The things that Paul has spoken are the abominations of desolations that are going on and taking place in the church now. These are the abominations of desolations spoken of by Daniel the prophet.

"The great tribulation and the rapture."

Sad to say, the saints think that they are going to be happy-go-lucky and not suffer through anything. The Bible tells us that when Jesus was in a fleshly body, he suffered in his flesh, and we are to arm

THE GREAT TRIBULATION

ourselves likewise to suffer. If we do not suffer in our flesh, we will continue to sin. The Bible said that suffering in our flesh will cause us to cease from sin. If we want to be like Jesus, we got to do as Jesus did. The Bible tells us in 1 Peter 4:1–2: "FORASMUCH THEN as Christ hath suffered for us in the flesh, arm yourselves likewise with the same mind: for he that hath suffered in the flesh hath ceased from sin. That he no longer should live the rest of his time in the flesh to the lusts of men, but to the will of God."

Jesus is giving us warnings that we should have our houses set in order. Stop the foolishness and the playing around as if time is in our control. We had better get in a hurry and get things in order now because, after a while, it is going to be too late. That which we do not have, we will not be able to run and get it, and if we can get it, when we make it back, it just might be too late. Jesus likened the kingdom of heaven unto ten virgins; five were wise, and five were foolish. That is the way that the church is: Part is wise, and part is foolish. The Bible said,

> THEN SHALL the kingdom of heaven be likened unto ten virgins, which took their lamps, and went forth to meet the bridegroom. And five of them were wise, and five were foolish. They that were foolish took their lamps, and took no oil with them. And the wise took oil in their vessels with their lamps. While the bridegroom tarried, they all slumbered and slept. And at midnight there was a cry made, Behold, the bridegroom cometh; go ye out to meet him. Then all those virgins arose, and trimmed their lamps. And the foolish said unto the wise, Give us of your oil; for our lamps are gone out. But the wise answered, saying, Not so; lest there be not enough for us and you; but go ye rather to them that sell, and buy for yourselves. And while they went to buy, the bridegroom came; and they that were ready went in with him to the marriage: and the door

was shut. Afterward came also the other virgins, saying, Lord, Lord, open to us. But he answered and said, Verily I say unto you, I know you not. Watch therefore, for ye know neither the day nor the hour wherein the Son of man cometh. (Matthew 25:1–13)

The example of the five foolish virgins who did not have any oil in their vessels who went to buy some, and when they returned, the door was shut, that is exactly what Jesus is telling us about that is leading up to the great tribulations and afterward.

The Bible went on to say, "Let him which is on the housetop not come down to take anything out of the house. Neither let him which is in the field come back to take his clothes. And woe unto them that are with child, and to them that give suck in those days!" To those that are with child and give suck in those days, Luke goes more into details as to what is going to be taking place in those days. It is written in Luke 21:22–23: "For these be the days of vengeance, that all things are written may be fulfilled. But woe unto them that are with child, and unto them that give suck, in those days! For there, shall be great distress in the land, and wrath upon this people." The Bible went on to say, "But pray ye that your flight be not in the winter, neither on the sabbath day." Talking about the flight not being in the winter, this calls to my attention how the children of Israel were in the wilderness for forty years, and for forty years, winter and the other three seasons came forth, and they wore the same clothes and shoes all those years. They could not go and get changes of raiment and shoes; likewise, we will not be able to do that either. Concerning the children of Israel in the wilderness for forty years, the Bible said, "And I have led you forty years in the wilderness; your clothes are not waxen old upon you, and thy sandals are not waxen old upon thy foot" (Deuteronomy 29:5).

"The world is about to enter into something that has never been here before, nor seen before."

The Bible went on to say, "For then shall be great tribulation, such as was not was since the beginning of the world to this time,

THE GREAT TRIBULATION

no, nor ever shall be. And except those days shall be shortened, there should no flesh be saved: but for the elect's sake those days shall be shortened" (Matthew 24:21–22). The saints of God are going to go through some tribulations and persecutions, but not as much as the ungodly; for our sake, Jesus is going to shorten the days.

We have got to know Jesus, and be known of him because false Christs and false prophets are coming forth, and they are coming forth with signs and wonders and working of miracles. Jesus tells us in Matthew 11:28–30: "Come unto me, all ye that labor and are heavy laden, and I will give you rest. Take ye yoke upon you, and learn of me; for I am meek and lowly in heart: and ye shall find rest unto your souls. My yoke is easy, and my burden is light." The Bible went on to say,

> Then if any man shall say unto you, Lo, here is Christ, or there; believe it not. Behold, I have told you before. Wherefore if they shall say unto you, Behold, he is in the desert; go not forth: behold, he is in the secret chambers; believe It not. For as the lightning comes out of the east, and shineth even unto the west; so, shall also the coming of the Son of man be. For wheresoever the carcass is, there will the eagles be gathered, together.

"We shall be raptured after the tribulation."
The Bible went on to say,

> Immediately, after the tribulation of those days shall the son be darkened, and the moon shall not give her light, and the stars shall fall from heaven, and the powers of the heaven shall be shaken. And then shall appear the sing of the Son of man in heaven: and then shall all the tribes of the earth mourn, and they shall see the Son of man coming in the clouds of heaven. And

he shall send his angels with a great sound of a trumpet, and they shall gather, together his elect from the four winds, from one end of heaven to the other. That is going to be a great day unto them, who has allowed him to wash them of their sins with his precious blood; and an awful day for them whose sins have not been washed away. Every eye shall see him, but only them who has been washed in the blood of the Lamb shall return to heaven with him. (Matthew 24:29–31)

The Bible said,

> And from Jesus Christ, who is the faithful witness, and the first begotten of the dead, and the prince of the kings of the earth. Unto him that loved us, and washed us from our sins in his own blood. And hath made us kings and priests unto God and his Father; to him be the glory and dominion forever and ever more. Amen. Behold, he cometh with clouds; and every eye shall see him, and they also which pierced him; and all the kindred of the earth shall wail because of him. Even so. Amen. (Revelation 1:5–7)

When Jesus shall return to gather, together his elect, and every eye shall see him, the dead in Christ, and also the dead that is not in Christ. The Bible said,

> But I would not have you to be ignorant, brethren, concerning them which are asleep, that ye sorrow not, even as others which have no hope. For if we believe that Jesus died and rose again, even to them also which are sleep in Jesus will God bring with him. For this we say unto you by the word of the Lord, that we which are alive and

THE GREAT TRIBULATION

> remain unto the coming of the Lord shall not prevent them which are asleep. For the Lord himself shall descend from heaven with a shout, with the voice of the archangel, and with the trump of God: and the dead in Christ shall rise first. Then we which are alive and remain shall be caught up together with them in the clouds, to meet the Lord in the air: and so, shall we ever be with the Lord. Wherefore comfort one another with these words. (1 Thessalonians 4:13–18)

It behooves us to live in and of the Lord Jesus Christ that if we should die before the return of Jesus to gather his elect, we will be in the first resurrection because the second resurrection has no power. The Bible said,

> And I saw thrones, and they sat upon them, and judgement was given unto them: and I saw the souls of the that were beheaded for the witness of Jesus, and for the word of God, and which had not worshipped the beast, neither his image, neither had received his mark upon their foreheads, or in their hands; and they lived and reigned with Christ a thousand years. But the rest of the dead lived not again until the thousand years were finished. This is the first resurrection. Blessed and holy is he that hath part in the first resurrection; on such the second death hath no power, but they shall be priests of God and of Christ, and shall reign with him a thousand years. And when the thousand years are expired, Satan shall be loosed out of his prison. And shall go out to deceive the nations which are in the four quarters of the earth, Gog, and Magog, to gather them together to battle: the number of whom is as the sand of the sea. And they went up on the breadth of the

earth, and compass the camp of the saints about, and the beloved city: and fire came down from God out of heaven, and devoured them. And the devil that deceived them was cast into the lake of fire and brimstone, where the beast and the false prophet are, and shall be tormented day and night for ever and ever. (Revelation 20:4–10)

"This generation shall not pass until all these things be fulfilled."

The end is drawing near, but the end is not going to come until all these things that Jesus has spoken shall be fulfilled. The Bible went on to say,

Now learn a parable of the fig tree; when his branch is yet tender, and puts forth leaves, ye know that summer is nigh. So likewise, ye, when ye shall see these things, know that it is near, even at the door. Verily I say unto you, this generation shall not pass, till all these things be fulfilled. Heaven and earth shall pass away, but my words shall not pass away. But of that day and hour knows no man, no, not the angels of heaven, but my Father only. (Matthew 24:4–36)

"This is the great tribulation that is to come."

Chapter 6

Who Shall Be Able to Stand?

I am concerned about people being able to stand in the latter days and during the great tribulation; but more so, and more than anyone else, I am concerned about me. When John was on the isle of Patmos, he was able to look upon the throne of God, and he saw the Lamb who had great wrath. In Revelation 5:5, he called him the Lion out of the tribe of Judah. John saw so much of his wrath loosed until it made him wonder who was going to be able to stand. So he asked the question in Revelation 6:17: "For the great day of his wrath is come; and who shall be able to stand?" When I read about the things that John saw coming into this world, I get worried and troubled about my soul. As I said, I want to help as many as I can to be prepared for that great day, but I am at the top of the list.

To be able to stand, we have got to do everything that the Bible tells us to do. The first two things we are to do is to present our bodies unto God, a living sacrifice, and to get our minds transformed. The Bible said,

> I BESEECH you therefore, brethren, by the mercies of God, that ye present your bodies a living sacrifice, holy, acceptable unto God, which is your reasonable service. And be not conformed to this world: but be ye transformed by the renewing of your mind, that ye may prove what is that

good, and acceptable, and perfect, will of God. (Romans 12:1–2)

When we present our bodies unto God, a living sacrifice, we are to become dead to sin and alive in God through Christ Jesus and not let sin reign in our mortal bodies to be obedient thereto. The Bible said, "Likewise reckon also yourselves to be dead indeed unto sin, but alive unto God through Jesus Christ our Lord. Let not sin therefore reign in your mortal body, that ye should obey it in the lusts thereof" (Romans 6:12). Once Jesus has delivers us out of our sins, he wants us to stand fast and hold fast to our liberty in him. Jesus tells us in Galatians 5:1: "STAND FAST therefore in the liberty wherewith Christ hath made us free, and be not entangled again with the yoke of bondage." Our liberty or salvation does not come unto us by any works that we do, but we are saved by grace. The Bible said, "For by grace are ye saved through faith; and that not of yourselves: it is the gift of God. Not of works, lest any man should boast. For we are his workmanship, created in Christ Jesus unto good works, which God hath before ordained that we should walk in them" (Ephesians 2:8–10). Because of the fact that we are saved by grace, that does not give us an occasion to sin. The Bible said,

WHAT SHALL we say then? Shall we continue in sin that grace may abound? God forbid. How shall we that are dead to sin, live any longer therein? Know ye not that so many of us were baptized unto his death? Therefore, we are buried with him by the baptism into his death: that like as Christ was raised up from the dead by the glory of the Father, even so we also shall walk in newness of life. For if we have been planted together in the likeness of his death, we shall be also in the likeness of his resurrection. Knowing this, that our old man is crucified with him, that the body of sin might be destroyed, that hence-

THE GREAT TRIBULATION

forth we should not serve sin. For he that is dead
is freed from sin. (Romans 6:1–7).

Once all those things have been done in our lives, God seals
them until the day of redemption. The Bible said, "And grieve not the
Holy Spirit of God, whereby ye are sealed unto the day of redemption" (Ephesians 4:30).

"Great Tribulations comes before redemption."

In the tribulation times, to be able to stand is to be strong in
the Lord. Paul tells us in Ephesians 6:10–11: "Finally, my brethren,
be strong in the Lord, and in the power of his might. He tells us
what to do to be strong in the Lord. Put on the whole armor of
God, that ye may be able to stand against the wiles (tricks) of the
devil." During tribulations and warfares, he lets us know what we
are wrestling against and what we are not wrestling against. It is said
in Ephesians 6:12, "For we wrestle not against flesh and blood, but
against principalities, against powers, against the rulers of the darkness of this world, against spiritual wickedness in high places." The
battles and the warfares that we are in and going to be in are spiritual.
For spiritual warfares and battles, it is going to take spiritual weapons. Paul said that we are not wrestling against flesh and blood but
against spiritual wickedness. So Paul tells us in 2 Corinthians 10:3–5:
"For though we walk in the flesh, we do not war after the flesh. (For
the weapons of our warfare are not carnal, but mighty through God
to the pulling down of strong holds)." Casting down imaginations
and every high thing that exalts itself against the knowledge of God
and bringing into captivity every thought to the obedience of Christ.

We have got to labor during these warfares, but God does not
want us laboring and building or laying our own foundations; if we
do so, we shall not be able to stand. The foundation has already been
laid. Jesus is that foundation who was laid by the prophets and the
apostles. Paul tells us to be mindful of how we build thereupon. The
Bible said,

For we are laborers together with God:
ye are God's husbandry, ye are God's building.

PASTOR CHRISTINE PEEBLES

> According to the grace of God which is given unto me, as a wise master-builder, I have laid the foundation, and another, builds thereon. But let every man take heed how he builds thereupon. For other foundation can no man lay than that is laid, which is Jesus Christ. (1 Corinthians 3:9–11)

Paul talked about himself being a wise master-builder, but he also let us know that the foundation was not laid by him alone. He told us in Ephesians 2:19–20: "Now therefore ye are no more strangers and foreigners, but fellow-citizens with the saints, and the household of God. And are built upon the foundation of the prophets and the apostles, Jesus Christ himself being the chief corner stone." John said, "I was in the Spirit on the Lord's Day, and heard behind me a great voice, as of a trumpet. Saying, I am Alpha, and Omega, the first and the last: and what thou see, write in a book, and send it unto the seven churches which are in Asia" (Revelation 1:10–11).

"The seven wraths and judgments to be loosed into the world." The Bible said,

> AND I saw in the right hand of him that sat upon the throne a book written within and on the backside, sealed with seven seals. And I saw a strong angel proclaiming with a loud voice, who is worthy to open the book; and loose the seven seals thereof? And no man in heaven nor in earth, neither under the earth was able to open the book, neither look thereon. John wept because no man was found worthy.

The Bible went on to say,

> And I wept much, because no man was found worthy to open and read the book, neither to look thereon. The Lion out of the tribe

THE GREAT TRIBULATION

of Judah, who has gotten full of the abominations, wickedness, and the sins of this world, he is beginning to roar, and who shall be able to stand?

The Bible went on to say, "And one of the elders saith unto me, Weep not; behold, the Lion out of the tribe of Judah, the root of David, hath prevailed to open the book, and to lose the seven seals thereof." John was beyond the river of Jardon baptizing, and the Bible said, "The next day John sees Jesus coming unto him, and saith, Behold the Lamb of God which taketh away the sin of the world" (John 1:29). Well, for tribulation times, he saw the Lion out of the tribe of Judah. Among all the tribulations, and for the saints of God who is making preparation to stand, John saw the slain Lamb among the four beasts. The Bible went on to say, "And I beheld, and lo, in the midst of the throne and of the four beasts, and in the midst of the elders, stood a Lamb as it had been slain, having seven horns and seven eyes, which are the seven Spirits of God sent forth into all the earth" (Revelation 5:1–6).

The Lamb is opening one of the seals. The Bible said,

> AND I saw when the Lamb opened one of the seals, and I heard, as it was the noise of thunder, one of the four beasts saying, come and see. And I saw, and behold a white horse: and he that sat on him had a bow; and a crown was given unto him: and he went forth conquering and to conquer. Him whom John seen on the white horse who went conquering and to conquer, that was the Lamb of God, the Lion out of the tribe of Judah.

The Bible said in Revelation 19:11, "And I saw heaven opened, and behold a white horse; and he that sat upon him was called Faithful and True, and in righteousness he doth judge and make war." The Bible went on to say, "And when he had opened the second seal, I heard the second beast say, Come and see. And there went out another horse that was red: and power was given to him that sat thereon to take peace from the earth, and that they should kill one another: and there was given unto him a great sword." Peace being taken away from the world was happening when Jesus was here in a fleshly body, and it is happening more so now. Jesus told us where we could find peace in this world of tribulations. The Bible said, "These things I have spoken unto you, that in me, you might me have peace. In the world ye shall have tribulation: but be of a good cheer; I have overcome the world" (John 16:33). When John saw men killing one another, that is happening every day and right now. Jesus talked about those things also, and what he was going to do before all flesh would be destroyed. The Bible said, "And except those days be shortened, there should no flesh be saved: but for the elect's sake those days shall be shortened" (Matthew 24:22).

The Bible went on to say,

> And when he had opened the third seal, I heard the third beast say, Come and see. And I beheld, and low a black horse; and he that sat on him had a pair of balances in his hand. And I heard a voice in the midst of the four beasts say, A measure of wheat for a penny, and three measures of barley for a penny; and see thou hurt not the oil and the wine.

Speaking of famine, I read an article dated October 5, 2023, saying, "Communities across Africa, including Kenya, Nigeria, Ethiopia, and Somalia, are facing the worse food crisis in decades; yet it is only just hitting the headlines." There is another type of famine that is already in existence that God said that he was going to send upon the land—that would be the famine for hearing the word of God. The Bible said,

> Behold, the days come saith the Lord God; that I will send a famine into the land, not a famine of bread, nor a thirst for water, but of hear-

THE GREAT TRIBULATION

ing the words of the Lord. And they shall wander from sea to sea, and from the north even to the east, they shall run to and fro to seek the word of the Lord, and shall not find it. (Amos 8:11–12)

The Bible went on to say,

> And when he had opened the fourth seal, I heard the voice of the fourth beast say, Come and see. And I looked, and behold a pale horse: and his name that sat on him was death, and Hell followed him. And power was given unto them over the fourth part of the earth, to kill with the sword, and with hunger, and with death, and with the beasts of the earth. John saw death and hell following him; well, the type life that we live shall determine what type life shall follow us after death, heaven, or hell.

Most definitely, death is coming; it is written in Hebrews 9:27: "And as it is appointed unto men once to die, but after this the judgment." Talking about death and hell followed him, there was a rich man in the Bible who died, and hell followed him.

The Bible said,

> There was a certain rich man, which was clothed in purple and fine linen and fared sumptuously every day. And there was a beggar named Lazarus; which was laid at his gate, full of sores. And desiring to be fed with the crumbs which fell from the rich man's table: moreover, the dogs came and licked his sores. And it came to pass, that the beggar died, and was carried by the angels into Abraham's bosom; the rich man also died and was buried. And in hell he lifted his

eyes, being in torments, and sees Abraham afar off, and Lazarus in his bosom. (Luke 16:19–23)

The question being asked, "Who shall be able to stand?" Lazarus was the one who was able to stand.

The Bible went on to say,

> And when he had opened the fifth seal, I saw under the altar the souls of them that were slain for the word of God and the testimony which they held. And they cried with a loud voice, saying, How long, O Lord, holy and true, dost thy not judge and avenge our blood on them that dwell on the earth? And white robes were given unto every one of them; and it was said unto them, that they should rest yet for a little season, until their fellow-servants also and their brethren, that shall be killed as they were, should be fulfilled.

I am almost certain that John the Baptist was one of them whom John saw under the altar that was slain for the word of God and the testimony that he held. The Bible said,

> For Herod himself had sent forth and laid hold upon John, and bound him in prison for Herodias sake, his brother Philip's wife: for he had married her. For John had said unto Herod, It is not lawful for thee to have thy brother's wife. "John the Baptist shall cry from the under the altar."

The Bible went on to say, "And immediately the king sent an executioner, and commanded his head to be brought; and he went and beheaded him in the prison" (Mark 6:17–18 and 27).

The Bible went on to say,

THE GREAT TRIBULATION

> And I beheld when he had opened the sixth seal, and, lo, there was a great earthquake; and the sun became black as sackcloth hair, and the moon became as blood. And the stars of heaven fell unto the earth, even as a fig tree casts her untimely figs, when she is shaken of a mighty wind. And the heaven departed as a scroll when it is rolled together; and every mountain and island were moved out of their places. And the kings of the earth, and the great men, and the rich men, and the chief captains, and the mighty men, and every bondman, and every free man, hid themselves in the dens, and in the rocks of the mountains; and said to the mountains and rocks, Fall on us, and hide us from the face of him that sits on the throne, and from the wrath of the Lamb. For the great day of his wrath is come; and who shall be able to stand? (Revelation 6:1–17)

The lion out of the tribe of Judah is about to be full. As I have read and learned about a lion, it does not start to roar until it has gotten full of its prey. Well, Jesus is that Lion out of the tribe of Judah, and he is angry and full. As John heard the people crying and saying unto the rocks and the mountains, fall on us, and hide us from the face of him that sits on the throne and from the wrath of the Lamb. Surely, all these things shall come to pass, and we need to get and do what it is going to take to be able to stand.

"Who shall be able to stand?"

When the seventh seal is opened, then we will find out that it is going to be the prayers of the saints, that shall cause them to stand. The Bible said,

> AND WHEN he had opened the seventh seal, there was a silence in heaven about the space of a half hour. And I saw seven angels which stood before God; and to them were given seven trum-

PASTOR CHRISTINE PEEBLES

pets. And another angel came and stood at the altar, having a golden censer; and there was given unto him much incense, that he should offer with the prayers of all saints upon the golden altar which was before the throne. And the smoke of the incense, which come with the prayers of the saints, ascended before God out of the angel's hand. (Revelation 8:1–4).

We, the saints of God, had better be praying the type prayers that were spoken of in James 5:16: "Confess your faults one to another, that ye may be healed. The effectual fervent prayers of a righteous man avail much."

Before the seventh seal was loosed, it had been told to us, who shall be able to stand. The Bible said,

AND AFTER these things I saw four angels standing on the four corners of the earth, holding the four winds of the earth, that the wind should not blow on the earth, nor on the sea, nor on any tree. And I saw another angel ascending from the east, having the seal of the living God; and he cried with a loud voice to the four angels, to whom it was given to hurt the earth and the sea. Saying, Hurt not the earth, neither the sea, nor the trees, till we have sealed the servants of our God in their foreheads. And I heard the number of them which were sealed: and there were sealed a hundred and forty and four thousand of all the tribes of the children of Israel. Of the tribe of Judah were sealed twelve thousand. Of the tribe of Reuben were sealed twelve thousand. Of the tribe of Gad were sealed twelve thousand. Of the tribe of Aser were sealed twelve thousand. Of the tribe of Nepthalim were sealed twelve thousand. Of the tribe of Manasses were sealed twelve thou-

THE GREAT TRIBULATION

sand. Of the tribe of Simeon were sealed twelve thousand. Of the tribe of Levi were sealed twelve thousand. Of the tribe of Issachar was sealed twelve thousand. Of the tribe of Zabulon was sealed twelve thousand. Of the tribe of Joseph were sealed twelve thousand. Of the tribe of Benjamin was sealed twelve thousand. The twelve tribes of Israel is what makes up the hundred and forty and four thousand that John seen the seal of God in their foreheads. After that vision, John seen a multitude who was clothed in white robes; those are the ones, that we, the true saints of God shall be numbered among.

The Bible went on to say,

And I beheld, and, lo, a great multitude, which no man could number, of all nations, and kindreds, and people, and tongues, stood before the throne, and before the Lamb, clothed with white robes, and palms in their hands. And cried with a loud voice, saying, Salvation to our God which sits upon the throne, and unto the Lamb. And all the angels stood round about the throne, and about the elders and the four beasts, and fell before the throne on their faces, and worshipped God. Saying, Amen: blessing, and glory, and wisdom, and thanksgiving, and honor, and power, and might, be unto our God for ever and ever. Amen. And one of the elders answered, saying unto me, What are these which are arrayed in white robes? And whence came they? And I said unto him, Sir, thou know. And he said to me, These are they that came out of great tribulation, and have washed their robes, and made them white in the blood of the Lamb. Therefore are they before the throne of God, and serve him day and night in his temple: and he that sit's on the throne shall dwell among them. They shall hunger no more, neither thirst anymore; neither shall the sun light on them, nor any heat. For the Lamb which is upon the throne shall feed them, and shall lead them unto living fountains of waters; and God shall wipe all tears from their eyes. (Revelation 7:1–17)

When I read in Revelation 7:14, "Washed their robes, and made them white in the blood of the Lamb, I said, Lord, I do not know how to do that; what am I suppose to do?" God gave me a reference that goes back to Isaiah 1:18: "Come now, and let us reason together, saith the Lord: though your sins be as scarlet they shall be as white as snow; though they be red like crimson, they shall be as wool."

"The great tribulation, who shall be able to stand? The ones that shall be able to stand, shall be them who have come out of great tribulations, and have washed their robes and made them white in the blood of the Lamb."

About the Author

At the age of five, Christine Peebles was taken in to the home of her grandparents in Swainsboro, Georgia. That is where she resided until adulthood. Christine felt the call of God upon her life since her childhood, but she did not understand what was going on. A broken marriage with two children to raise alone, with many hurts, pains, and other troubles that comes along with life—those were the things that helped her to find her way to the cross.

Christine was born again on September 25, 1975; and immediately, she began talking to God, and God talked to her. God told her that he was giving her the gift of prophecy, and within three weeks, he began prophesying through her. For over forty-eight years, God has spoken through her prophetically concerning things that were to come to pass.

God called Christine into the ministry on August 5, 1981. She worked the works of an evangelist and went out on the streets, people's yards and into their homes, and tent revivals until God called her into pastoring in April 1998. She is now operating in three ministries, pastoring, evangelizing, and prophetic. God told her, "I'm giving you the ministry of reconciliation."

Christine's testimony (book) I Overcame by the Blood of the Lamb caused people to talk to her about things that they could not talk to anyone else about. Even as she was overcome by the blood of the Lamb, her testimony caused others to overcome.

Contacting the Author

Christine Peebles
P.O. Box 191
Swainsboro, Georgia, 30401
Phone (478) 237-7116
Victory Temple Ministry of Reconciliation
P.O. Box 914
Swainsboro, Georgia, 30401
Phone (478) 419-3968
OR-Email at peebleschristine@yahoo.com
OR website at http://www.pastorchrsitinepeebles.com